Good Advice

Printed by:
Tri Star Visual Communications
Phoenix, Arizona
January, 2005

Design & layout: Kinetix Group, LLC.
480.206.1445 • www.kinetixgroup.com

About The Cover

One of the final tasks in completing this work was the design of a cover, obviously one of the most important. I was almost completely bereft of ideas. It was my wife, Sue, who happened on the picture of our daughter, Ann E. (front cover), and half-seriously suggested I incorporate it to depict the book's message. She knew it was one of my favorite pictures and why.

At each *day* of our children's birth, Sue said something prophetic about each (three) of them – something that bore true and remains true. For Ann E., the prophecy was, "This kid knows exactly what she wants and *she's strong*!"

The picture remains one of my favorites, as it seems to capture that determined look on her face. Her grip on the kitten leads me to believe we were probably trying to get her to put it down for some reason. Her response can be read in her eyes. They communicated (and still do 22 years later): "I've heard your *Good Advice* and I ain't buyin' it! One word from you and I'll do just as I please."

Sue and I are only half joking when we tell others, "Had Ann E. been able to drive a car at the age of three, she wouldn't have needed us at all." I'm sure she was not yet three the last time Sue dressed her. Indeed she did and continues to know exactly what she wants, and she's strong. People laugh when I describe her as "our chainsaw with feet!" Despite the challenge in raising a strong-willed child, I'm thankful for her tenacity. She'll need it in this world.

Ann's look is easy for me to recognize, as I've seen it in my own eyes, and I've heard it described many times by my sisters. It said, "Leave me alone, I know what I'm doing and I don't need your help or advice." Truth was, and is, I *did* need the help and advice of others. I sense young Ann E. is coming to that truth also, but about 23 years earlier than I did.

I liked the idea of this determined look in the eyes, as I'd guess many parents and spouses have seen and see it every day. It's a look that says, "*Good Advice* is not welcome here." If you can relate to this and know someone with this quality, suggest my book to them. Someday they *may* grow into it as many people do. If you see the look in *your* mirror, congratulations, you're growing – and don't *read* this book, *study it*, because it's an accumulation of much of the good advice yours truly ignored – mostly to my own peril!

Gratitude & Dedication

There are so many people I could and eventually will thank for help in getting this book into readable form.

I want to begin by expressing my gratitude to the parents and staff of the Caledonia Middle School in Michigan. After fifteen years in central office administration, I returned to work with the middle school children I love so much. Most of you have no idea the confidence and encouragement you provided me with your casual comments about the weekly columns (*Thursday Thoughts from The Principal*) I would write. I would be remiss not to express a special gratitude to Mrs. Judy Skinner and Mrs. Mary Duba, as they were the ones who looked at my work every week and made suggestions that would help the readers understand what I was trying to say. If any of you people are reading this – thank you from the bottom of my heart for expressing your appreciation for my work. It is the single most important factor in my belief in my writing.

Sharon Machoul is a determined woman who took who took a class from me in Phoenix, AZ. She learned I was struggling with finishing and publishing a book and said to me, "Craig, here is a phone number, call Neil DeCarlo. He is a writer and will help you." One year later, Sharon took another class from me and came up to me very first thing and said, "You didn't call Neil DeCarlo!" There was a look in her eye that spoke clearly, so, following that class, I called Neil and we met. Thank you, Sharon, for being firm with me. This was exactly the push I needed.

Mr. Neil DeCarlo, my editor, was a phenomenal help to me not only in technical suggestions, but also with his encouragement for my writing. Through Neil, I met Scott Farmer of Kinetix Group and Chris Sicurello of Tristarvisual Publishing, both in Phoenix. Scott did the designing of my cover and page layout and Chris orchestrated its becoming book form. While their work is of extreme quality, what I appreciated most about Neil, Scott, and Chris is who they are – genuine, sincere human beings. Their first interest was in me as a person – an interest so vital yet in such short supply in today's world.

My gratitude goes to the children God placed in my care. Notice I didn't refer to them as my children. This is because I don't believe I can own another person, including children. I loved and cared for them, often with fault, but never with ill intention. I thank them because of the lessons they taught me as I observed their growth. Since childhood, one of my goals was to give children a start in their lives as the person I tried so hard to become since age 40. I don't think these children realize (or believe) how much they taught their father as early as the first day of their lives. A sincere, bottom-of-the-heart thanks goes to Craig H. II, Steven M. and Ann E., Schmidt.

I love Phoenix, Arizona and have come to love so many of the fine educators there. I began working there in 1998 simply because I was looking for a warm climate to do a little work in my retirement. I never dreamed I'd meet so many wonderful people in the process. Thank you for appreciating my work as a teacher and for giving me hope that the children of Arizona are in such good hands. Those of you who have come to know me understand how important this is to me.

Finally, thank you to my wife, Suzanne. One of my all time favorite songs is by Bette Middler. Its title is *My One True Friend*. In it she describes the one person in her life who stuck with her and inspired her through thick and thin. My wife, Sue, is my one true friend. As is normal, in our 30-plus years of marriage, we've had our ups and downs, but our love for one another and our dedication to raising children who would be committed to the welfare of the world was never a question. While my confidence in myself has gone up and down over the years, her confidence in me never wavered and was often all I had to lean on and go forward. She will always be my one true friend and I can't thank her enough for her dedication to me and to my work.

It's to all of you I dedicate this, my first book. I want you to know how thankful I am for the contribution you made to it, each in your own way.

Very Sincerely,

Craig Schmidt

Middleville, Michigan, April, 2004

"When a true genius appears in the world, you may know him by this sign, that the dunces are all in confederacy against him."

Johnathan Swift

Table of Contents

Forward

I learned about the author of this book, Craig Schmidt, through a mutual acquaintance. Craig was seeking a little editing help, and our mutual friend knew I was a writer. She recommended that Craig and I meet to discuss his book and how I might help him bring it to completion.

Craig shared his "good advice" with me – the culmination of his thinking and teaching for many years. As I sat with him and talked, it didn't take me long to realize that the advice in this book is as much a product of experience as it is of sound principles.

As a school administrator and long-time educator, Craig has extensively interacted with many people, parents and young people. The more I spoke with him about his experiences, and his passion to make a difference, the more I got to know a man who truly cares.

Still, I wondered about his manuscript, *Good Advice*. I hadn't yet read it, and, admittedly, I was predisposed to think it would be a relatively feeble attempt to characterize wisdom – just because so many "self-help" books are.

But then I began to read Craig's book, and it struck me deeply with its simplicity and selflessness. Is good advice the kind that challenges a person to change – to become more empty of ego and more filled with compassion?

That's the type of good advice Craig gives in his book, and he does it in a way that makes you want to be a better person – to listen more than talk, care more, reach a part of yourself that's been overrun by the more material and time-bound aspects of modern life.

Good Advice takes you out of the material and temporal realm and helps you journey into the spiritual and timeless dimension. It's not feeble by any definition and, in fact, it's a rarely unfiltered view into the struggles and strengths of what it means to be human.

With his stories, research and brutal honesty, Craig shows you – as he showed me – what it means to experience yourself as a vessel of genuine goodness in the world.

Craig is a person who doesn't want to gain anything in life beyond such goodness, and his interactions with me have been nothing less than completely consistent with this desire. How rare it is to meet someone like this and have the blessing of his presence in your life.

How rare, too, that a book is written only from the spirit of giving, and of leaving the world a better place. My good advice to you: read this book and take it to heart. It will change your perspective.

Neil DeCarlo,

Fountain Hills, Arizona

Author's Preface

My father (Henry Schmidt) and I were walking home from the store one cold winter night when I realized I had forgotten my mittens. Even though I was only three or four years old, I had an inner sense of how to solve problems that has stayed with me over the years.

I decided I would unzip my jacket and put my arms inside it so my hands would stay warm. He didn't say why, but my dad advised me not to do it. I persisted, so he zipped up my jacket after I removed my arms from the sleeves and placed them close to my chest. Problem solved, and we continued on our way.

It couldn't have been five steps later I hit a patch of ice and went down face first. My inability to break the fall meant my nose was the first thing to hit the icy ground, and I bled like a stuck pig. "I told you so, " my father said. "Next time, pay attention to what I tell you."

> **"You won't like the celery fields, son."**
> Henry Schmidt

Years later, my folks made me pick blueberries to earn money. It paid six cents per pint, and I earned anywhere from $2.40 to $6.00 per day, depending on how hard I was willing to work and the quality of the berry crop.

I hated picking blueberries. I hated working hard. I deduced that if I could find a job that paid by the hour, I could at least escape the "working hard" part of the job: be a bit more relaxed and still get paid.

My friend worked in a celery field for fifty cents an hour. I begged my dad to let me work there instead of going to the blueberry patch with my mom. My dad advised me, "You won't like the celery fields, son. It's much harder work than picking blueberries." What does he know, I thought. He's never picked blueberries. What I didn't know was my dad *had* worked in a celery field!

You already know the end of the story. Of course his advice was right, as dads always are. After two weeks of getting out of bed before the chickens, a case of celery rot on my hands and a tyrant for a boss, I gladly rejoined my mom and sisters in the blueberry patch.

So went the first two instances I can recall in my life when I ignored *Good Advice*.

In the years since these early lessons, I've figuratively "fallen face down" scores of times. Many of the "stories" you are about to read describe what I learned after my "nose stopped bleeding" from all the falls. I've come to wonder if any lesson can be learned other than the hard way, through experience. I can recall many instances when I rejected *Good Advice* and proceeded with *My Plans*. It wasn't until middle age that I discovered, *The Problem With Good Advice Is It Usually Interferes With My Plans!*

Despite this discovery, and at the same time because of it, I wrote my first book and filled it with - *Good Advice*. Any wisdom you find herein came to me the hard way. Strange, I spent most of my life *ignoring* good advice, then wrote a book called *Good Advice*. I have no explanation for this except that I believe certain of my words and stories can spare others from the high "rent" I paid for my ignorance and hardheaded allegiance to my own plans.

I'm thankful that reaching "middle age" began a tremendous journey of growth in my life. I resent the "mid-life crisis" label, as this implies a lost soul chaotically searching for meaning, even as the soul itself grows gray. I think "mid-life epiphany" comes closer to describing my experience. It's been a mysterious, illuminating and, most of all, exciting time of life for me.

I'm thankful you've decided to let me share these small parts of my journey, as your journey can't be too much different than mine. We are all human, and we all have hope for greater happiness. Sometimes a little *Good Advice* is all we need to get to the next level of growth and self-discovery. Knowing someone else has stumbled over the same stone as you helps to ease our burden, too.

Hold your beliefs and understandings up to the light. Open your mind to the possibility that there may be other ways. *Make* yourself grow. This is the best way to ensure an epiphany instead of a crisis – *at any age*.

My hope is that you'll never finish using this book, even if you do finish reading it! From my heart, I hope it helps you, even if it's in a small but important way. Helping others has always rewarded me, and I only ask that, in return, you help someone else.

Sincerely,

Craig Schmidt

"When It Fits Like That"

During a visit with an orthodontist, my wife and I were weighing the possibility of correcting a small, congenital defect in our son's upper and lower jaw alignment. The doctor had cast a mold of the young teeth and was showing us how the two jaws didn't align as they should. He first showed us how it was (imperfect) then how it should be (perfect).

It was very clear to me how he kept going back to the plaster cast and emphasizing the perfect position. It was obvious when the jaws were not meeting perfectly that the doctor became uneasy and uncomfortable. When the jaws fit perfectly, his body was relaxed and comfortable.

The orthodontist caused me to recall a story told by one of my favorite authors, Don Clifton. Dr. Clifton told of a discussion with a cabinetmaker who described how he put together two pieces of wood to make a door for a cupboard. He cut the pieces to show Don. The fit was so close to perfect one could hardly tell it was two pieces of wood. "Don", he said, "In order to be a good cabinet maker, you gotta feel good when it fits like that!" (Clifton 1998)

> **"…Mister, it just ain't gonna shine like it should"**

So it was with the orthodontist. He was a quality craftsman who cared for his patients, especially their teeth. I looked at him after about the fifth time he held the cast jaws in front of our faces and said, "You know, Doc, you gotta feel good when they fit like that!"

A huge smile overcame his face as I'd described exactly what he felt. He'd never heard it put that way. I couldn't help but wonder if he was having an epiphany. Maybe my comment sparked a discovery, or maybe he was smiling simply because he knew I "got it." I think he just liked being reminded of why he loved being an orthodontist so much and why he was such a good one.

Once I spilled some peanut oil on one of my shoes and it dulled the shine. After failing to recover the shine, I decided to have a professional shoeshine at the Grand Old Opry Hotel in Nashville. There were two shoe shiners working together and it was easy to tell they loved their jobs. They chattered and sang as they worked.

I sat in a chair and one of the men began to work on my shoes. He did the good shoe first and it shone beautifully. In tackling the soiled shoe, he soon began to sweat. He worked and sweat until he was mentally and physically exhausted. Finally, he said, "Mister, you musta spilled something on this shoe. It just ain't gonna shine like it should." He was dejected.

I told him it was peanut oil and he told me the shoe was worthless; it would never shine. But oh how he tried before he gave up on it. Less than perfect upset him. It was his love, his passion, his work. It is what "fit" for him.

Ignoring *Good Advice*, I worked many years at a job I didn't like; it didn't *fit*. How fortunate you are, I learned, if your work, "fits like that." If your work doesn't fit, listen to my *Advice*. Prepare to find work that does! ◆

Take Criticism Calmly
- even if you don't deserve it

Edward M. Stanton, Abraham Lincoln's Secretary of War, once called Lincoln "a damn fool." Lincoln was meddling in military affairs by signing an order moving some regiments to please a greedy politician. Stanton refused to carry out the orders.

Hearing this, Lincoln said, "If Stanton said I am a damn fool, I must be, for he is nearly always right. I'll just step over and see for myself." Stanton convinced him of his mistake and Lincoln rescinded the order.

A "non-defensive" nature has value few understand. A snake defends itself with its poisonous bite, a cat with her claws. Human evolution has led us to rely on our reasoning ability. "Being right" is often our defense. "Being wrong" renders us vulnerable to our "predators." Becoming non-defensive requires sacrificing the need to be right. It strips us of one of our main defenses.

> If enough people say you're drunk, go home.

Several years ago, I forced myself to develop the ability to say, "You're right, I'm wrong," without hesitation. I found I had to overcome my ego, my need to be right all the time and to admit it to the world. Letting go of that need was one of the most effective skills I've ever acquired.

In my college days, I loved to write and believed I was a good writer. I was gifted with a command of the language. I didn't earn it; I was given it. I delighted in finding new words and using them to communicate my thoughts.

My early writing was colorful – at least I thought so. However, I was advised to use fewer and simpler words. A friend helped me with some editing one time and, when finished, I hardly recognized the work as my own. I thought it read more like an instructional manual for a new lawn mower than the theme on peer counseling it was. This angered me, but my friend was an accomplished writer, so I examined my writing style. I determined he was right and I changed. That simple. Since then I try to make my points with fewer and simpler words. I'm grateful for my critics.

While a sustaining belief in myself kept the fire for writing burning, it was my ability to be non-defensive that allowed me to hear the advice I was getting. A defensive posture would have prevented the improvement I needed.

I see people bristle at suggestions given them for almost anything and they do so at their own peril. A defensive nature will discourage people from helping you. Retain a belief in yourself while remaining open minded to feedback from the outside. Ben Franklin said to be thankful for your enemies, as they are the only ones who will tell you the truth.

The finest gems in the world begin as shapeless rocks. The hands of skilled craftsmen (critics if you will) bring out the rock's natural beauty. Critics can be the craftsmen to reveal your natural ability. Allow them to do their work. Lincoln did! ◆

What's Wrong With This Picture?

Many years ago, on the front page of our local newspaper, there was a picture of the city's mayor and a second grade boy. The short description under the picture told that the mayor had visited class and had written something on the board. The lucky boy spotted a word the mayor had spelled incorrectly. How eager we are to recognize and praise people who look for *what's wrong*.

> **Great minds discuss ideas; average minds discuss events; small minds discuss people.**
> Adm. Hyman Rickover

We've all felt the sting of subtle criticism. "Why don't you wear your hair like Karen's?" "That's a lovely blouse but red isn't really your color." "I only tell you that because I love you so much." Need I go on?

In my teachings, I often show an overhead of one of the familiar, "What's Wrong With This Picture" exercises. I break the class down into groups and have them work on listing all that is wrong with the picture. Busily, they almost always make it into a game or a contest despite the fact that I purposely never announce it as either.

I sit back and observe the "fun" people have finding things that are wrong. As they near the end of their searches, they are even more excited to find yet one more thing. It's fun and they want to keep going.

> **No statue has ever been erected to a critic.**
> Jean Sebelius

I heard of a study wherein people were asked to tell about the marching band that had just gone by. Nearly 85 percent of the comments were similar to: "The clarinets were out of tune, the drums were not in line, the director's coat was ripped," etc.

An explanation by Richard Farson {1996} saddens me.

While we may think we are motivated by hearing about the success of others believe it or not, little is more encouraging or energizing than learning about or witnessing another's failure, especially if it is an expert who is failing. [p. 113]

He says most of us would rather hear of someone's tragedy or misfortune than their good fortune. Why is it that we have a difficult time jumping up and down for our neighbor who just won the lottery? Why do we prefer to hear of her difficulties or failings?

Maybe Gore Vidal captured at least part of the reason when he said, "When my friend succeeds, a little part of me dies." [Farson, p. 115]. While these words may bear some truth, they make me a little nauseous.

As I strive toward my ideal, I will find genuine excitement in the good fortune of other people. It saddens me to think I may be lonely when I get there. ◆

Just What <u>Would</u> Jesus Say?

These days, it's common to see people wearing bracelets bearing the initials, W.W.J.S. (What Would Jesus Say). This has its roots in the philosophy known as the Ideal Observer Theory. When I struggle with a decision between right and wrong, the silent mantra, "What would Jesus do?" usually helps me. It can also settle a lot of disagreements between people.

I lost one of my sisters in middle age. She was 50, she had been ill, but didn't let on the nature of her illness. Her sudden death and subsequent knowledge of the cause was reason for even greater suffering than normal at the loss of a loved one.

Since her death was sudden, her funeral arrangements and service were rushed. She belonged to a particular synod of the Lutheran Protestant religion that has several different synods. The synods have different rituals and ceremonies and beliefs about the general Lutheran faith.

> **Preach Christianity. And if you must, use words.**
> St. Francis of Asisi

Our family was raised in a small Lutheran church where my brother in law, Bill, was the organist, a phenomenal organist. He played at our home church as a teen and continued to play in a church wherever he lived for fifty years. Incidentally, he is probably the nicest man I've ever met.

My sister's funeral was held at her childhood church (Bill's also) but the church she attended, a different synod, ran it. Same Lutheran Church, different synod. Bill, of course, offered to play the organ for his sister in law's funeral. The old folks of the town would have loved that, not to mention the rest of my family. However, he wasn't allowed to because, in their synod, only a member could play at a service. Lutherans of differing synods, in fact, aren't welcomed to the altar or to share in communion.

> **The problem with most Christians is they are so unlike their Christ.**
> Ghandi

I learned of this many years after my sister's death, from a trusted friend. I was angry and could have debated the injustice of not allowing Bill to play the organ. Instead, I said to my friend, "Just What Would Jesus have said?" It was over. He couldn't respond to that. Later, I learned from the Bible exactly what Christ would have said. In short, Christ would have said, "Bill is a Christian. Maybe he's not exactly like you, but he's one of us, he's a believer. Let him play the organ!" Gandhi said, "The problem with most Christians is they are so unlike Christ!" I guess this is a good example of that.

One doesn't need to know much to live a noble life. Generally accepted rules of civil human behavior are easy to find. If you happen to be Christian, the Ten Commandments are simple, few, direct and believable. Understanding the rules is easy; obeying them is the challenging part.

When facing a difficult decision, ask yourself, "Just What Would Jesus Say?" You may be surprised how obvious the answer can be! ◆

If I'm Patient, I Can Wait Faster

During their famous expedition across the Northwest Territory, Lewis (of Lewis and Clark) became ill and couldn't go on. They were somewhere in the Mississippi River Valley, so a messenger was sent to Washington to explain the delay to President Jefferson.

The best available method of delivering a message back in 1804 was a fast horse. Two weeks later the weary horse and rider arrived at the White House to announce that illness had temporarily halted the expedition. Thomas Jefferson thanked the messenger, fed and quartered him for the evening and sent him back with the message, "Take care of yourself and continue when you are able."

Two weeks later (one month total) the messenger returned. The poor horse died from exhaustion and the explorers were gone (long since resuming their expedition).

I'd like to contrast this with a frustration I experienced one hundred and ninety six years later! I was on the internet looking for a piece of research on 'time." I was corresponding with someone in Zurich, Switzerland. It must have taken all of thirty five seconds to send the message electronically. Fidgeting, I thought, "Geez, this computer is slow."

This struck me like a lightening bolt. It took Meriwether Lewis two weeks to get a message halfway across the North American Continent, and I was impatient that it took me thirty-five seconds to get a message half way around the globe!

I believe the statement, "all of man's problems stem from his inability to sit quietly in a room alone" is true. Many have lost a grip on time – if we ever had one. Because of technology, we've come to believe the human capacity to do more is limitless. It is not. The human "machine" is designed to do just so much. The capacity to "do" varies with the individual – but not by as much as we might think. Deciding how much we should "do" merits thought.

> **All of man's problems stem from his inability to sit quietly in a room alone.**

Western society puts tremendous pressure on us to do and acquire more. This has created an impatience that blankets our daily lives recognizable from our freeways though our phone lines right on to our kitchen tables (for those families who even have one anymore). Our health is the sacrifice we make if we choose to comply with these demands to do, be, and get more.

Notice how often (and where) you hear the phrase, "real quick." It seems nobody wants to take time. This pervasive impatience is fueled by the illusion that more things will make us happy. Quickly obtained *things* won't make us happy; rewarding relationships and time well spent with loved ones will. This requires patience and investment of time and self.

I think it was Aristotle who said, "A fool is happy when his cravings are satisfied; a wise man is happy without reason." Happiness requires an ability to slow the pace of our lives, finding satisfaction with what we have, not with what we crave. A staple ingredient in the recipe is patience. Like it or not, there is no "real quick" way to patience. The shortest pathway is to develop the ability to sit quietly in a room – alone. This will not allow us to live longer, necessarily, but better. I hate it when I'm a fool! ◆

Life is a Video
- not a snapshot

I've learned some great things reading the backs of tee shirts. One on the back of a six year old said, "Be patient; God is not done with me, yet!"

Many walk around taking "snapshots" of things and situations believing they depict reality. Sometimes they take snapshots of others and conclude this is how people are – frozen as if real life was but an image on a piece of paper.

Fortunately, life is not like a photograph. Life is fluid like a movie moving from one scene to another in seamless fashion. A video, like the old movies, is thousands and thousands of photographs that, strung together, produce a flowing life story - one for each of us.

With so many billions of "snapshots" in the average lifetime, any *one* of them is at least deceiving, and at most destructive to the character.

Is that your final answer?

To see the "story" or "movie" of others requires the same patience the little boy was asking for with his tee shirt. Unfortunately, few practice the patience necessary to hold our judgment until enough snapshots have been taken to form an accurate picture of one's character.

In his poem titled simply, "If," Rudyard Kipling advises us to, "treat triumph and defeat as the imposters they are." Imposters! Come to think of it, triumphs and defeats are snapshots. They are temporary events at a point in time that may or may not be representative of the total being. In fact, failure is a vital and recurring aspect of any success story.

Aristotle suggested we be neither too happy in good times nor too sad in bad times, for life is ever changing. Happiness and sadness, different sides of the same coin, are only snapshots, imposters.

Understanding the "video nature" of life has helped me practice more understanding and less judgment. In the popular television show "Who Wants To Be A Millionaire?" contestants are asked, "Is that your final answer?" When I catch myself passing judgment on someone's behavior (snapshot) I ask, "Is that your final answer?" For me, the answer is always, "No." ◆

Force Doesn't Work

While driving my car one evening, I heard the news that a particular world leader announced a new "get tough" policy with a neighboring nation. My drive ended at a restaurant where I was going to enjoy a quiet dinner and do some writing.

Entering the restaurant I was seated next to a family of three - mom, dad and a teenage girl. They were having a fight. Since they were embarrassingly loud, it was clear the girl wanted to do something over the weekend and her parents objected. In the standoff the mother said, "I'll show you; you can just forget having Dana overnight this weekend."

"I don't care," responded the girl, "I'll still get to see her at the volleyball game." Of course, this couldn't be the last word so the mother said, "Maybe we won't even show up at the blankety-blank volleyball game." This embarrassed the father so he ended the confrontation by changing the subject. Everyone in the restaurant began enjoying dinner.

Early in my teaching career, I believed I could make children behave by scaring them. Fear would ensure the quiet attention I needed to teach American history. I practiced this belief until I heard a speaker named Bill Page prophetically declare, "If you are relying on fear and coercion to teach your class, you aren't very good at all!"

Despite my youth and inexperience, his statement had a huge impact on me. I began practicing "no threat, no fear" teaching the very next day. While this was more challenging, it was, I believe, my first day as an effective teacher.

> I grabbed his shoulder and began squeezing it, he grabbed my tie and began pulling it. . .
>
> Craig Schmidt

When I became an assistant middle school principal, I found that the need to "make" kids behave was much greater than it was in the classroom. A school full of adults expected me to make students behave. I reverted to the belief that force, threat and fear would work. I recall the specific event that reversed this old belief – again.

Young Steve was not behaving to my expectations. His continual disruption of his classes was unacceptable, and I had to do something about it. In my office, the young man and I had an exchange similar to the exchange between the young girl and her parents in the restaurant. I could tell my words weren't having much effect on Steve so I walked around my desk to get closer to him. I grabbed his shoulder and began squeezing it. He grabbed my tie and began pulling it. I was stunned. I didn't know what to do so I intensified my grip. I'd show him.

(Continued on next page)

He pulled harder on my tie. I tried one more time with my patented "triple-flex Nelson" grip! You guessed it. Steve had a new grip of his own that he exercised on my necktie.

Thankfully, I calmed down and let go of his shoulder. He let go of my tie. I sat back down and, at that very moment, began a new career as a principal. Force, threat, intimidation and fear, I concluded, do not work. I don't care if it is dealing with young Steve in the principal's office, young Janice in the restaurant or two feuding nations. While fear and force may appear to be effective, their effects are short term, and the best result is usually temporary minimal compliance – threat gone; compliance gone.

Following a student shooting incident at a San Diego area high school, the principal addressed a group of parents and said that the school's modern and elaborate safety precautions failed them. He said they would turn their focus to the relationships between students and adults.

This is another admission that strategic plans, force, fear and armament don't work. We need to begin focusing on the relationships between one another. In almost every case of school shootings, the shooter(s) feel(s) excluded, teased, humiliated, etc. by other students.

Mahatma Gandhi said, "If there is going to be world peace, we need to start with the children." I hope I live to see the day when there is a worldwide initiative to reach all children. If there is ever going to be world peace, all children need to learn that our only hope is focusing on human relationships. Children must learn to believe that, regardless of race, religion, national boundaries, high schools, etc. they need to respect and include one another.

Dwight D. Eisenhower said,

"Every gun that is made, every warship launched, every rocket fired signifies a theft from those who hunger and are not fed, those who are cold and not clothed. Money spent on arms is not only money spent. It is spending the sweat of its laborers, the genius of its scientists, the hope of its children." (Edelman 1992)

In 1842, Abraham Lincoln spoke of leading and influencing others:

When the conduct of men is designed to be influenced, persuasion, kind, unassuming persuasion, should ever be adopted. It is an old and true maxim that a drop of honey catches more flies than a gallon of gall. So with men. If you would win a man to your cause, first convince him that you are his sincere friend. Therein is a drop of honey that catches his heart, which, say what he will, is the great high road to his reason, and which, once gained, you will find but little trouble in convincing his judgment of the justice of your cause, if indeed that cause really be a just one. On the contrary, assume to dictate to his judgment, or to command

(Continued on next page)

his action... and he will retreat within himself, close all the avenues to his head and his heart...Such is man, and so must he be understood by those who would lead him. (Decker 1992)

When I see pictures of twelve-year old children holding machine guns, it suggests to me some cultures are teaching their young that problems can be solved using force, violence and hatred. These means will secure short-term compliance at best. They will never gain the heart of another. They simply steal food, clothing and shelter from the children they love.

Force doesn't work in our neighborhoods, our schools or our world. ◆

Believing In Yourself

In my experience as a deputy superintendent of personnel and labor relations, as well as my stints as a middle school principal, I had numerous situations that required courage, persistence, calm and confidence - usually all at once! Near the end of my career, a teacher admired these qualities and asked me how I became as confident as I was; how did I instill such a strong belief in myself?

Her specific question was "How come these attacks don't bother you?" I saved the e-mail. I modified it a bit, but below is my response to the teacher.

> **You don't have to live in Harlem when you grow up.**

Truthfully, it still bothers me a little when this happens, but the time it resides with me is down to minutes. I am not perfect and I know where my shortfalls are. I own up to them. Basically, I believe in myself. I care about other people and rarely try to hurt people, intentionally. However, there are times when I intentionally try to hurt people. It's interesting, and I will explain that if you stop in my office sometime. But for the most part, I love and want to help other people.

I believe this about myself, Jeannie: I sincerely believe that if Christ came to me and I asked him to give me one bit of advice, He would say, "Craig, I want you to help my children in any way you can." Therefore, if I am helping (and I believe I am), I figure any judgment people pass on me is not very important. I am even willing to help the ones who cast the stones. That's the long answer. The short answer is that I like myself and have a strong belief in my value to do what I believe Christ most wants me to do. How did you like it? I also want to add that I don't see myself as a very religious person. I'm not into Christianity as humans designed and practice it. While I believe strongly in the concepts of Christianity, I don't believe Christ would attend church (regularly) if he came back to earth. I also find it extremely curious that, in the Old Testament of the Bible, it says God repented for making man (Just before he contracted with Noah to build an ark as he was going to destroy all of mankind). Hard to say all that without sounding churchy but I'm not a "churchy" person! My admiration of Christ has more to do with the fact that he was such a great guy than it does with the belief, held by many (myself included), that He was the son of God.

A healthy belief in self is mandatory for growth to take place. If we believe we have a say in our own future, a feeling of optimism will prevail in our lives. This optimism sustains us and provides the drive for us to prosper.

I remember listening to a sixth grade teacher from Harlem. He described his class of kids as: inner city, impoverished and unmotivated. He said he would be

(Continued on next page)

happy if he could teach his children only one thing all year long…they didn't have to live in Harlem when they grew up. To most children in Harlem, the future is dim, threatening and, worst of all, predestined. They believe there is nothing they can do to alter it.

Viktor Frankl, eminent psychiatrist, said, "It is a peculiarity of humans that we can only exist by looking to *our* future and this is *our* salvation in even *our* most difficult times." Sr. Charleszetta Waddles, American writer, said: "You can't give people pride, but you can provide the kind of understanding that makes people look to their inner strengths and find their own sense of pride."

Adults have the power to instill belief in young people. Children want to look up to adults and gain their approval. The most important work teachers can do is help children believe in themselves. This can be a challenge because so many students score poorly on state-mandated and other standardized tests. It's been said that you can measure the speed of a horse with a stopwatch, but it takes a race to measure its heart. A child's self-belief is measurable by his or her accomplishments in the race of a lifetime, not by a test score. ◆

The Maverick

The definition in the box below was found in The American Heritage Dictionary. Looking up the word, "dissent" I found, "A state of disagreement and disharmony - difficulty, conflict, friction, contention, clash, strife, dissension, discord, dissonance, variance, dissidence." Wow! This is a host of descriptors many parents use to describe their children!

Actually, more people have maverick tendencies than we recognize. Children, sensing they are out of the mainstream, and unwelcome, often suppress their true personalities. How sad because, throughout history, it is the maverick personalities that advanced the frontier of knowledge. They are the Einsteins, Edisons, Picassos, Dennis Rodmans and Beatles of the world. They are the ones whose self-values were strong enough to carry them through the criticisms and ridicule to which many mavericks are subjected.

Most children are not that strong.

Notice that the first definition of a maverick is "An unbranded range animal, especially a calf that has become separated from its mother, traditionally considered the property of the first person who brands it."

> • **maver-ick - n**
> 1. **An unbranded range animal, especially a calf that has become separated from its mother, traditionally considered the property of the first person who brands it.**
> 2. **One that refuses to abide by the dictates of or resists adherence to a group; a dissenter.**
> • **mav-er-ick adj. - Being independent in thought and action or exhibiting such independence.**

"Unbranded" people rarely belong to a particular group of thought or action. Yet the world is filled with parents, teachers, managers, etc. who tirelessly try to "brand" these kids and get them to conform to particular thoughts or actions. They mean well, they are often frustrated.

A skilled teacher or coach can accept a different (often difficult) personality, nurturing it carefully, to both teach it and extract from it the phenomenal ability locked within. Destined for failure is the teacher, coach or parent who cannot accept these children for what they are and, instead, persist in making them mainstream, normal, domesticated.

While comparisons often find Asian and European students superior to American students, it has been our history of acceptance and cultivation of maverick tendencies that has vaulted the United

(Continued on next page)

States to a position of global economic and social prominence. When compared with others, our culture encourages our young people to "think out of the box," and this type of thinking is the cornerstone of our progress.

However, it is critical that someone with a maverick personality understand and accept his/her responsibility for his/her behavior. We live in a fairly traditional, linear and logical world. Like anyone else, maverick personalities need to learn to adapt to this reality. Failure to accept it can result in endless hassles with society's penalties for non-conformance.

The maverick's life is better if he/she learns to adapt to a more conventional style when the situation calls for it. Likewise, when in "safe" territory, it is time to "let their colors show." Suppressing talent inhibits growth.

If someone close to you has a maverick personality, cherish it, as it usually comes with tremendous talent and ability for greatness. Help him/her understand his/her uniqueness, how to know when to display it and when to conform to the expectations of the general society. Attempting to "brand" them will suppress the greatness in their destiny. ◆

What's Wrong With US?

Is American society in trouble as some of our allies around the globe are suggesting? I'm uncomfortable with what appears to be evidence that we are in trouble. Whether it is an individual, a society or a race of people, I believe it necessary to self examine. Let me give some examples of why I feel it would help America to do a little self-examining.

In his book, *Simple Truths, Vital Lies*, (1985) author Daniel Goleman states, "The people in power are distant, uninformed and indifferent to the perils of the middle class and the impoverished. The middle class and the impoverished lack power." At America's formation, French philosopher DeToqueville stated, "If a manufacturing aristocracy gains control of our government it will be the worst form of tyranny man has ever seen."

I believe recent discoveries of corporate greed, graft, fraud and outright thievery robbed us of trust in business executives (the people in power), revealing a dangerous proximity to the condition DeToqueville cautioned against (manufacturing aristocracy controlling government)

> The biggest problem with American society isn't haves and have-nots. Nor is it the biggest problem the ever-widening gap between the haves and have-nots. The biggest problem we face is so many of the haves don't care if the have-nots ever become haves. Worse yet, some of them strive to see it never happens.
>
> C. Schmidt

But "Main Street" America is not faultless in its contribution to this dangerous condition. I make no bones about having little respect for a "manic wild man" style of coaching. Media and entertainment, to satisfy our appetite for victory, have made this turbulence, violence and lack of respect for others center stage – front page. This style embodies the evil many have come to idolize on their obsessive path to win at any cost. It exemplifies our willingness to sacrifice our dignity and integrity (the value we place on ourselves) to be #1. Of course, I'm not speaking of every American but, painfully, too many of us and the ones to whom our media panders.

Cheating, graft, political sway, fraud are merely milder forms of "manic wild men" as well as testament to our desire to win at any cost. They are evidence that many of our "manufacturing aristocracy" are looking for an easy road to riches, unwilling to earn it the honest hard way.

A questionable media mentality continues to direct our country's moral development. A formidable influence, the entertainment industry has a huge influence

(Continued on next page)

on the development of our youth. Daytime soaps, for example, contain suggestive moral messages far more graphic and decadent than the "X" rated movies I sneaked into when I was a youth. This is dangerous for our society since children are developmentally unable to interpret these moral (immoral) messages.

We've come to worship idols in models, athletes and Hollywood movie stars. Placing second in anything is to be branded, "loser." Cheating, scandals and drug abuse among athletes are so normal that they are losing their front-page billing. Sadly, we've come to accept them as a part of a typical ascension to the top.

To be healthy, I believe Americans need to be willing to at least examine our image as the rest of the world sees us. Some view us as an arrogant "manic coach" recklessly pushing, shoving and stepping on others on our way to the top. This approach has never lasted in history and never will. The "little guy" will only be stepped on for so long. He will eventually prevail because of his sheer numbers.

There is an old African proverb that says, "If there is no enemy inside you, the enemy outside you can do you no harm." I question the fear of many American's to look inside. I love America as much as anyone you will ever find. I love why and how we were formed. But I fear we've become dangerously different than the original intent of our founding fathers. In order to see this, we must expose ourselves to a careful examination of what we value, what we hold as ideal and how far away from those two we might have strayed.

Ignoring, denying or covering up problems in a wave of patriotism and pride is as unhealthy for us as a nation as it is for me as a single American. I need to be open to how I project myself to others as, undoubtedly; the world will reflect it back to me. The same is true for all of us. ◆

Let It Go

I've found that few people understand the meaning of forgiveness. Most believe the purpose of forgiving is to relieve someone else of the responsibility for a hurt they caused. Forgiveness is actually a tool of healing essential to *our* mental health.

William James, considered by many as the father of modern psychology, said, "I could free eighty percent of the people in mental institutions if I could teach them to forgive." He was referring to people unwilling to let go of the past, especially their pain. They continually dwell on old hurts and transgressions consuming most of their time, unproductively.

Get Over It!

Contentment lies not in what happens to us, but how we react to it. Many react to their past by refusing to let it go. They hold tenaciously onto the past as if it soothes them. But the effect of holding on is just the opposite; it causes sickness. Some seek an audience on which to dump their grief; others (more dangerously) hold it in, stewing quietly. Either way is devastating to the spirit.

I can't change reality but I can determine my reaction to it! "No one can rewrite their past but anyone can write their future, everyday." It helps me to reason there is little I can do about my past. It's over, I've hurt others or been hurt and that's it. I must let it go. I must focus on my future, applying any lessons from the past. It's like the rear view mirror in my truck. It's good to glance where I've been once in a while, but my real interest and safety is in where I 'm going.

When I had a dog, I accidentally stepped on his tail. He yelped and ran away from me only to return moments later for his normal attention. Almost instantly, he'd forgiven me. Psychologists tell us if we haven't let go of something within eight minutes, we are holding on to it – and causing anguish. My dog could have told me that!

I recall a story told by Earl Nightengale. A woman lost her only child (a daughter) to a violent crime and, for eighteen years, she was in and out of mental treatment facilities seeking relief from her angry, bitter, vengeful feelings. Relief, she thought, would be in the execution of the man who created all her pain. Holding on to these feelings for eighteen years was her reaction to the crime, and it consumed her. Her salvation came when she visited her daughter's murderer on death row and forgave him. Her well being was restored; her spirit was healed. I can't offer stronger evidence of the healing power of forgiveness.

(Continued on next page)

No creature on earth (other than human) punishes itself more than once for a mistake! It's important to emphasize that we must forgive *ourselves*. When we make mistakes we need to apologize where necessary and move on. As damaging as anything are the repeated "beatings" we give ourselves for past mistakes. Also, if your thinking is filled with "should 'ofs' or should haves:" get over that, too. It's done and you need to move on. I said it's *important* to emphasize this point; I mean it's *critically important* to emphasize it.

If you sense a spiritual discomfort – a dis-ease – take a look inside and see if you're holding on to things; if you're unwilling to forgive. Let them go, get over it, forgive. You may be ignoring what could be the key that unlocks the gate to your pathway of spiritual health. ◆

Just Be Nice

Among psychiatrists there is a belief that states, "Technique is something that is relied on until the real psychiatrist arrives (Palmer)." It means that the effectiveness of a psychiatrist is more a function of the quality of the person than the skills and techniques learned in training.

I've noticed a trend in employee friendliness. There seems to be a sincere, "Hello" at the door and a, "Can I help you" around nearly every corner in the super stores. Business seems to have learned that the biggest factor of customer satisfaction is a friendly, helpful atmosphere. If customers are treated and welcomed pleasantly, they will return to the store.

> Be kind for everyone you meet is fighting a hard battle.
>
> Plato

What business has learned has long been known about individuals. Men like Dale Carnegie spoke of this years ago in his epoch book, *How To Win Friends and Influence People*. I just finished the book and its main message is simply, be nice.

Self-improvement requires gathering "baseline data." This means a look inside to determine how others see us. This can be painful, which explains our reluctance to do it. If objectively done, however, we will have critical "data" for our improvement.

The answers to some simple questions will give us a good start to seeing ourselves as others see us. Might be a good idea to ask a trusted loved one to answer the questions for you.

- Do you look for the good in people?
- Are you quick to criticize?
- Do you give to people who can give you nothing in return?
- Are you selfish?
- Do you gossip?
- Are you sensitive and gentle in your approach?
- Do you hold grudges?
- Are you optimistic?
- Are you positive?
- Are you loyal (even to those who are absent)?

(Continued on next page)

- Are you trustworthy?

- Are you dependable?

- Do you read quality literature?

In his book, *Leading Quietly*, Joseph Bedarraco gave the example of a manager at work that was advised to fire a worker whose performance was lacking. Instead, the manager spoke with the worker – a single mother with two sick children and money problems. The manager chose to make the employee's work life more accommodating to her personal problems. This solved the problem of the employee's work quality and met an employee's personal needs at the same time.

The manager was "just being nice." My mother in law used to say this to us all the time. Funny how we listen better if a college professor writes a book about it, yet the best lessons of our lives come from the people we respect. Sometimes (in fact most times), they might be housewives or grandparents!

My idea for this piece of *Good Advice* came when I observed a girl on a student bus trip snap at a boy who asked her how she enjoyed the park. The popular girl snapped, "Cedar Point Stinks!" This was not true. She was saying to him, "Don't talk to me. You aren't worthy of my time. How cruel she was and how much good she could have done just by being nice. I don't think people realize the power they have to encourage others to grow.

I'm happy to report the idea of being pleasant seems to be catching on. As business seems to have discovered the "value" in being nice, I see our schools also beginning to spend a small bit of their resources on character education. I look for this to grow. ◆

Lots of Reasons; No Excuses

When we are faced with a tragedy such as the Colorado school (Columbine H.S.) massacre there are many more questions than answers. One question everybody asks is, "What can be done to prevent tragedies such as this?"

> ... the very things we value as Americans cause much of the malicious, criminal behavior we see.

First, it must be said that there is no excusing this behavior – no excuses. However, I learned in Psychology 100 at Western Michigan University that every behavior has a reason behind it. What reasons would cause two young men to commit such an invasive, abusive "theft" of so many hopes and opportunities? We must answer this question to help us feel safe in our surroundings.

Some aberrant behavior is likely due to genetic reasons. Experts study and debate this endlessly. While we cannot deny or do much to prevent genetic causes, it is important to recognize they are a small percentage of the problem.

Most agree that all the perpetrators of such crimes are different, often loners and alien to the mainstream of what we term normal. To varying degrees and in different ways, each of us fit these different, loner and alien descriptors. We all have experienced the sting, hurt and drain of exclusion and rejection.

I remember an awful feeling I had in second grade. Five or six of the "poor" children (we knew who we were, even at that age) and I were made to stand in front of the gym class and tell the other thirty children why we didn't have gym shoes. How embarrassed, worthless and hurt I felt as I told the class that my father was laid off and we couldn't afford shoes. Understand me, I am not losing sleep over this and I live a wonderful, plentiful life. Now and then, I feel just a tinge of the exclusion, rejection and hurt many feel every day. It is similar feelings, accumulated over fifteen, eighteen, or forty years that cause some to scrap any respect they might have for fellow humans and avenge these feelings of anger, hurt, rejection and worthlessness. They turn to senseless, often indiscriminate acts of violence.

In his book, *Management of the Absurd*, Richard Farson (Farson 1996) says the very things we value as Americans cause much of the malicious, criminal behavior we see. Many people in America lack access to the "good life." Further we (you and I), unknowingly, contribute to their condition. Here are some of the ways.

(Continued on next page)

In our schools:

We provide curricula and reward systems that are narrow and exclusive. Curricula, grading systems and award systems are designed to recognize and reward only a small percentage of our population. Daily, schools fail to meet the needs of *most* of the students. After thirty-three years in public education, I'd say schools fail to adequately service eighty percent of their students. This is rejection and exclusion in its worst form, and it is so preventable.

In our communities:

We help out only when we benefit or profit. For example, I coached soccer teams when my children were on the team. Why don't I do the same thing when my children are *not* on a team? The painful answer to this question led me to our local middle school, where I took on the mentoring of a young man who was having problems in school. I had nothing to gain (so I thought) from doing this. The feeling of helping another person grow is reward in itself.

In our churches:

Some, when looking for a plumber to fix their drains or a contractor to build their house will only consider someone who attends *their* church. Many prefer to live and otherwise contract only with those who think, raise their children and act as we do. Their patronage is familial, religious or local. Too many are unwilling to endure any discomfort to accommodate someone with differing ways, from a different culture. Some allow their church to do their thinking and determine their behavior. Loyalty remains with the church instead of the nation to which we belong or to humanity itself.

Krishnamurti said the things we allow to divide us – our gods, our nationalism, our selfishness, our prejudices, our gender, our ideals – are the very things that cause wars and other violence in the world. Things that divide us cause two normal babies to live eighteen years, then go into their high school and murder thirteen of their classmates and themselves. They probably saw life as worthless and hopeless.

All human beings have basic needs to be understood, appreciated, validated and affirmed. We will go to nearly any length to have these needs met. Some will even desperately resort to killing one another for them. ◆

Managing Anger

There is plenty of literature explaining how to control anger, but most of the advice is the same. Suggestions follow the lines of "restraint, calm, refrain, stop, count, pause, think, etc.

Most people understand what it is they *should* do to curb their anger. What I have never seen is the *how* to do it. When that burning inside me begins, that rapidly growing fire inside my chest, how do I prevent myself from doing or saying something I'll regret a short time later? I *know* what I am supposed to do (refrain, count, pause, etc.); I lack the control to employ it!

> Feeling angry is beyond our control; acting angry is fully within our control.

Can I delay my urge to buy things I want? Can I hold my tongue when someone offends me? Can I leave some food on my plate at the end of each meal? An understanding of my emotional or limbic brain is necessary to answer these questions. Often called the "fight-or-flight" brain, the actions this part of the brain controls are involuntary or reactive. Thought, contemplation and premeditated are not terms used to describe its functioning. Restraint, counting, pause, stop, etc. involve passage of time – also a foreign concept to the limbic center. Simply, the limbic brain just *acts and acts quickly.*

Unlike other organisms of the earth, however, humans have some ability to restrain their emotional (limbic) brain. I am not saying humans are able to control (hence the term, "restrain") our fight-or-flight brains. What we can control are our thoughts and behavior.

Feeling angry is beyond our control, but acting angry (or not) is fully within our control. Humans have a thinking brain called the cerebral cortex that, with will and practice, can delay the actions of the limbic (emotional) brain. There is no magic or secret in this. It is a simple matter of will and practice. One must have the knowledge, the belief and the will – but even these don't guarantee full control.

Count on setbacks. It's important to forgive yourself when you fall short of your ideal. Move on, apologize where needed, and get over it! Most of all, believe that you can manage your emotional reactions if you recognize them and work to restrain them using your abilities of reason and choice of reaction (often inaction). ◆

Getting The Rocket
Off The Ground

I read that over 90 percent of the energy required to send the first men to the moon (and back) in 1969 was expended lifting the rocket five hundred feet off the ground! This is less incredible to me if I picture my average day. Often, nearly ninety percent of my mental energy is spent to get my feet on the floor and body into the shower. I've tried tricks to make this easier. I tried leaving the obituary section of my newspaper next to my bed so I could glance at it in the morning to see if there was anyone listed with whom I'd care to switch places. But that was too much hassle.

To energize for my day, I need a good start. I like to spend forty-five minutes to an hour at a local coffee shop (preferably near a window) with a strong cup of dark roast coffee. Solitude, coffee, maybe a bagel and a soothing book or page of writing, are the balm I need to overcome the "pain" of getting out of bed. When I awaken, a mental picture of my coffee shop and a slight body stretch help me get my feet on the floor.

Writing takes a lot of my energy. For this reason, I avoid it. I easily find other things to do when I know I should be finishing a book. Starting to write is even more difficult for me than getting out of bed.

Julia Cameron's book, *The Right to Write* (Cameron), has influenced my *will* to write more than anything and remains one of the few books I have read twice.

> The moment
> one definitely
> commits oneself,
> then Providence
> moves, too.

In browsing my notes from her writing, I noted that Julia writes even when her mood is bad and she doesn't feel like writing. This was my feeling the day I penned this chapter. Cameron urges to "just begin to write and follow where it goes." This is the "trick" to get going, despite my mood, and it is not exclusive to writing. Just getting started works for everything.

Some days my mood is not only "I don't feel like writing today;" some days my mood is, "I don't feel like 'lifing'." My spell checker suggests, "lifing" is a new word. To say I don't feel like "living" sounds suicidal and I've never felt that. When I don't feel like "lifing," I lack the drive and the energy to face my problems and stresses (including and especially finishing this book).

Famous philosopher, Goethe said, "Whatever you think you can do or believe you can do, begin it. For action has magic, grace and power within it." Similarly, mountain climber William Hutchinson Murray said, "Concerning acts of initia-

(Continued on next page)

tive or creation, there is one elementary truth, the ignorance of which kills countless ideas and splendid plans: that the moment one definitely commits oneself, then Providence moves too."

Thomas Edison said, "Success is one percent inspiration and ninety-nine percent perspiration." In difficult, challenging or just normal times in your life, these time-tested laws of nature will bring Providence to your side.

It is important to remember that most of the fuel is required just to get the rocket off the ground and you must provide the spark for ignition! The spark is doing something. You must do something. ◆

Managing Depression

Working in my office one night, I decided to stop and go to bed. I went downstairs and said good night to my wife, who asked me, "Why so early?" I said to her, "My entire day hasn't gone well. Not terrible, but not well. It's best I just go to bed and try my luck again tomorrow." After thirty plus years of marriage, Sue understood and asked no further questions. I've lived with myself for well north of fifty years and, long ago, learned to recognize a particular day as a down day for me. I was experiencing a bout with the mild depression that's been in my blood since birth. I'm aware that, in my family of origin, manic-depressive illness (also known as bipolar) exists.

> **Recognizing the mood, the feeling, the dark blanket obscuring the sunlight from my day...**

I've recognized and lived with this mild depression well before I knew its medical name. I recall my father's symptoms (behaviors) associated with depression. While he seemed unable to overcome its effects, I feel blessed that I've been able to recognize them and employ techniques to overcome this potentially devastating disease.

Observing the damage this disease wreaked on my parents' and siblings' relationships, I vowed early in life to avoid situations where I'd seen the effects of depression raised havoc. Forty years into my life, I was pleased to learn that mental health experts (psychiatrists) recommend the same tools I developed on my own to deal with bouts of depression! Scott Peck addresses depression in several of his books (1978, 1993)

My most reliable weapon for this affliction is absence! Recognizing the mood, the feeling, the dark blanket obscuring the sunlight from my day, I act quickly (and discretely) to isolate myself from others. My moods don't last long, rarely a whole day. One of my first and most reliable indicators is a diminished tolerance of others. Things I normally take in stride will quickly annoy me and I find it difficult to redirect my focus. I also feel blessed that this occurs infrequently, maybe once every other month. It's not always easy to isolate myself physically but I have learned to isolate myself psychologically by *avoiding* situations, people and issues that create conflict. This takes a strong will and emotional control. I'm always regretful when I am in a down mood and engage in a conflict and thankful when I restrain myself.

In my teachings of stress management, I speak openly and unapologetically of my mild depression. I am not responsible for its presence in my nature, but I am responsible for how I behave. My behavior is my choice. People used to keep depressive tendencies "in the closet" because it was associated with insanity.

(Continued on next page)

They feared being labeled "crazy." Saturnine and melancholy were gentler, more acceptable terms used to describe the disease. Fortunately, secrecy and denial are no longer accepted means of dealing with depression. It surprised me, at first, how many students (adults) would thank me for talking openly about my genetic propensity to experience depression. Some seem relieved to confide they (or their spouse) are affected by depression and it helps to hear someone talk about it without reservation, embarrassment or apology.

I've also read professional literature on bi-polar. Kay Jamieson's book, *An Unquiet Mind* (1994) is an excellent resource. I learned there are cases of such severity that no amount of positive thought, mental gymnastics or other "self" means provide relief. Modern medicine has discovered chemical origins for the bipolar disease, and some people suffer from chemical imbalances that defy any means other than one of the variety of newer anti-depressant medications. Anyone who has attempted self-help without success should consult a physician to determine a possible need for medication. I would do that in a heartbeat.

I heard of a case of a woman who was severely depressed. After years of prayer, etc., she visited a physician and began a program of prescriptive medicine for her condition. Her husband was an extremely outgoing, gregarious, positive, "live on the sunny side of the street" type of person. When her medication began to have its uplifting effect, she sat up on the bed one morning and said to her husband, "This is how you feel all the time, isn't it? I have never felt this way in my entire life." The twist to the story is that, shortly after experiencing this elevated mood, she left her husband and joined a traveling band! Both of their lives are on good tracks again even though they are no longer husband and wife.

Lack of awareness precludes a remedy for depression. Relief for depressed feelings lies in recognizing them, admitting them and employing whatever means necessary to overcome them. ◆

Open Your Mind

In a recent conversation with a friend, I was reminded of one of the biggest problems I see in the world. We were discussing our differing beliefs about religion and life. I have learned to listen to people to understand them, especially if I don't agree with them. I see the truth in Steven Covey's (1989) "First to understand, then to be understood" concept. People appreciate it when someone listens to them; it's a form of loving them.

> **Jesus died to take away your sins; not your mind.**

I listened to my friend's belief first. He was rather emotional, passionate and dramatic. While I didn't agree with him, I listened to understand him.

Next it was my turn. I wasn't a sentence into my explanation when he interrupted me. I excused myself and told him I wasn't finished. He let me continue, but I couldn't complete three sentences in a row without either a verbal interruption or a look on his face that said as clearly as the written word, "I ain't even gonna try to understand this!"

I did finish my explanation of my belief, eventually. However, it was crystal clear that my friend made no attempt to understand me, much less agree with me.

I find his reaction to me not only common, but a major problem in our world. People pick up beliefs and refuse to open their minds to anything else. This is dangerous. While there has probably always been a shortage of open-minded people, I'm certain they have been the ones responsible for progress. I'm sure we have open-minded, examining people to thank for automobiles, steamships, moon travel, etc. – since they were the ones open to new ideas, not slaves to old beliefs. Many great inventions began as folly – the work of eccentrics not to be taken seriously. Closed minds are the brakes on the progress that has made us a world leader.

The word education has its roots in the Latin word, "educere" which means, "to draw out." To be educated, I need to open up my eyes and my mind to search for truth in the world. I can do this. I must do this. I can begin by listening to beliefs other than my own with an open mind. ◆

Dick and Cora

I am a nice person. Some people dispute that and there are times they are right. Years ago, I decided I wasn't nice enough and determined to be a better person. I did this by learning what nice people do, altering my actions whenever I behaved differently. With this knowledge it became easy to spot behavior that wasn't nice.

One of the things I learned about nice people is they are appropriately humble. When nice people teach at a university, as I do, they are kind to and interested in all the different types of workers at the university. They learn the names of the custodians and security workers, as well as the deans of the colleges. They are genuinely interested in them as they would be the people who supervise them. I emphasize: genuinely.

> **Dick continues to enjoy his job; Cora is gone.**

When I arrive early in the morning on Saturdays, Dick is often the guard on duty. He always greets me with a smile and, "There's a fresh pot of coffee in the workroom." I love coffee in the morning, and Dick feels good about brewing it for me and the other teachers.

Recently, there was a new guard on duty, a middle-aged woman. I'll call her Cora. I greeted her as I greet Dick and the others. While polite, her greeting was less than enthusiastic. To make conversation, I asked Cora if there was any coffee left in the workroom. "I just got here," was her response in a mildly defensive tone. Cora isn't quite as excited as Dick about making coffee for the employees. I emphasize "for the employees," because I believe a part of what makes Dick nice is his interest in doing things for others.

It was obvious Cora didn't take care of herself very well, either. She was usually tired and unkempt. She spent a lot of time reading a novel. It was not unusual to go by her and find her head down, napping. She did not appear to be a growing person. Dick, on the other hand, keeps himself neat and is always looking his best. What you see first and most is his general embracing of his life, his job and the people who come through the door. I learned from one of my students that Dick is a security guard at her high school and people love him there, too. This is no surprise; Dick is a nice person.

Helping other people for no reason other than *it is the right thing to do* is as valuable as anything I know. Caring about others is something I believe and, as Don Clifton once told me, I am supposed to do. I believe humans are social beings and we are supposed to care about other people. Plus, as Clifton added, "It works."

(Continued on next page)

In a recent trip to campus, I asked if Cora was on duty that weekend. "Cora was let go," responded the guard. I understood why. Cora was not a mean person. She was friendly and responded kindly to small talk. However, it seemed she had less interest in projecting a genuine smile and sincere interest in the people who came by her station than did her colleague, Dick.

The bottom line of the Dick and Cora story is: Dick continues to enjoy his job; Cora is gone. This is a powerful message to me. ◆

"Cause I Don't Want To!"

One day as a middle school principal, I was sitting in a meeting with a parent, a student, a director and two teachers. The student wouldn't do his schoolwork. The adults had their say as we described his problem. The boy's father finally asked why he wasn't doing his work. With his head down, the boy solemnly declared, "Cause I don't want to!" Completely frustrated, the father said, "I quit."

The student's candor combined with the father's reaction struck me as hilarious but I struggled to contain my laughter. This was a perfect example of a classic problem shared by almost everyone. We simply don't want to.

> ...we find ourselves putting things off or neglecting them totally, simply because we don't want to do them

Our meeting was called to discuss this young man's unwillingness to do his work. What can anyone do to someone who doesn't want to do anything? What quality of work can we expect from someone who doesn't want to do it?

In my 27 years as a school administrator, I can't tell you how many days (not hours) I spent in meetings because children weren't doing their work. I was a part of setting up contracts, behavior plans, agendas, calendars and so on - all of which avoided the real problem of "I don't want to!" Despite all our experience, we don't know what to do. Our old favorite, coercion, yields only minimal compliance. When a bad grade is no threat to the student, we've taken our best shot and missed.

The young man's response struck me so that I asked the adults in the room, "Were any of us like Joey when we were his age? Are any of us like that right now, where much of our daily work is a struggle and we find ourselves putting things off or neglecting them totally, simply because we don't want to do them?" Only one of the adults (besides me) admitted that he was just like that at Joey's age, and that was the boy's father. He said it was late in his life when he decided to buckle down, and he was always sorry he didn't do it sooner.

Doing things we don't want to do requires love. To me, love involves harnessing the *will* to extend oneself or put forth the effort to overcome what DeToqueville termed man's natural tendency to drift toward idleness. M. Scott Peck, in his famous work, *The Road Less Traveled* (Peck 1978) also talks extensively about man's natural tendency to be lazy. Overcoming laziness, says Peck, requires an effort called love. Learning to love means overcoming the temptation to do nothing. It is not easy.

(Continued on next page)

Why bother? Why not just do the things we want? Simply, we won't be happy with ourselves. We will leave no legacy. It is not death we fear but that we'll be remembered for little or nothing.

When I say to myself or someone else, "I don't want to," I am often describing my true feelings, and that is sufficient answer for me or anyone else. Sometimes, however, I need to see if the "I don't want to" response is foreclosing on something I want badly.

At the moment, I am near the end of nearly seven hours of editing this book. I began my day by saying to myself "I don't want to work on this book." I had to overcome that feeling and put forth the effort. Peck describes this effort as similar to love. I had to *will* myself to do something despite my feeling of "I don't want to." So many things in my life are like that. How about yours? ◆

Just Take a Pill

Watching television early one Sunday morning, I saw a woman dealing with serious symptoms from injections she took to lose weight. I noticed commercials on the same program advertising pills for weight loss, anxiety relief and arthritis pain.

In parts of Tibet, unusually low rates of prostate cancer are attributed to a diet high in soy protein. I learned this on a commercial advertising a pill that will give me similar protection against prostate cancer. I can live as recklessly as I want and just take their pill! This is what we're teaching our young, but it's not true.

Our society is a world leader in solving problems. We have solved the problem of transportation with the automobile, space travel with rocket ships and eggs sticking to frying pans with Teflon and Pam! We've come to believe we can cure all our illnesses, physical and mental, by taking a pill. We believe it is *natural* that the cure for our afflictions of mind and body are but a pill away. I've learned there is a difference between "treating" and "healing." Pills treat but, for the most part, we must do our own healing.

DePak Chopra (1993) contends our body is a self-enclosed pharmacy capable of producing all of the chemicals necessary to maintain and heal itself, mentally and physically. I believe it is natural for humans to live anxiety, pain and excess-fat free. The Mexican in the following story has as good a "pill" as I've seen for living free of disease. Trouble is, it's not for sale! Enjoy!

An American investment banker was at the pier of a small coastal Mexican village when a small boat with just one fisherman docked. Inside the small boat were several large yellow fin tuna. The American complimented the Mexican on the quality of his fish and asked how long it took to catch them.

The Mexican replied, "only a little while."

The American then asked why didn't he stay out longer and catch more fish?

The Mexican said he had enough to support his family's immediate needs.

The American then asked, "but what do you do with the rest of your time?"

The Mexican fisherman said, "I sleep late, fish a little, play with my children, take siesta with my wife, Maria, and stroll into the village each evening where I sip wine and play guitar with my amigos. I have a full and busy life."

The American scoffed, "I am a Harvard MBA and I can help you. You should spend more time fishing and with the increased proceeds, buy a bigger boat. With the proceeds from the bigger boat you could buy several boats, eventually you would have a fleet of fishing boats. Instead of selling your catch to a middleman

(Continued on next page)

you would sell directly to the processor, eventually opening your own cannery. You would control the product, processing and distribution. You would need to leave this small coastal fishing village and move to Mexico City, then LA, and eventually to New York City, where you will run your expanding enterprise.

The Mexican fisherman asked, "But, how long will this all take?"

"Fifteen to twenty years," the American replied.

"But what then" asked the Mexican?

The American laughed and said that's the best part. "When the time is right you would announce an IPO, sell your company stock to the public and become very rich; you would make millions."

"Millions," said the Mexican, "Then what?"

The American said, "Then you would retire and move to a small coastal fishing village where you would sleep late, fish a little, play with your kids, take siesta with your wife and stroll to the village in the evenings where you could sip wine and play your guitar with your amigos.

When you finish laughing, the veracity of this story will hit you. Then you might feel a little sad! The "treadmill" many of us find ourselves on between the beginning and ending of this story can be a sad awakening.

I hope I live long enough to experience the discomfort of, say, arthritis, and I hope I can maintain a mental and physical lifestyle that will provide me with comfort similar to the wise old Mexican fishermen. I will leave it to the Harvard educated MBA's of the world to sustain our economy, then fill their grocery carts with pills to solve the health problems they create by *their choices.* ◆

The Ethics of Life
-and the enemy within

In today's (7/21/02) news, much of the talk is about the ethics (or lack thereof) in business, specifically business executives. Our country's economy has been nearly wrecked since September 11, 2001, when terrorists struck icons of the American way of life, the Twin Towers of the World Trade Center and the Pentagon.

Our government and capitalistic business methods were figuratively and literally bombed. This accelerated an already existing downward business spiral. More devastating than the physical attacks on our society has been the exposure of a gross shortfall of ethics among many of our business leaders. In short, we've uncovered a bunch of crooks, cheats and thieves running our country's biggest businesses – the businesses that were figuratively and literally bombed on September 11, 2001.

> **Show me a dollar bill and I'll show you a crook.**
> Big Fred Scheffler

Today's newspaper has an article describing a fairly typical view of the general population. The title of the article is, "MBA Students Will Get The Ethics Message In The Wake of Scandals." There seems to be a lot of talk lately about how to teach ethics to our young, how to teach them to be honest.

I don't think the MBA program at the University of Michigan or any other place can teach young people to be ethical, honest or caring. This is a culturing, nurturing process that takes place in the formative years – or it seldom takes place at all. Still, I am enough of an optimist to believe that ethics, honesty and caring can be a choice made by a mature person, but it is a choice.

I can choose to be a more ethical person. First, if change is to be genuine or authentic, it must be made by someone who *deeply believes it is the right thing to do.* I emphasize this point because so many believe the best way to teach ethics and honesty is through warnings of punishments awaiting violators; behave only so you won't risk paying the consequences.

Fear of consequences is *not* the right reason to be honest or ethical, but it is the most popular one! When I look inside myself and don't like what I see, then I *might* make a genuine change. But this change must take place *inside of me,*

(Continued on next page)

and not simply because of fear of outside consequences. There is an old African proverb that states, "If there is no enemy inside you, the enemy outside you can do you no harm."

In the 1950s Nikita Khruschev of the Soviet Union warned the United States, "We will bury you." Everyone thought he meant militarily, so we increased our fortifications and defense budgets. We hurried to protect ourselves from the *enemy outside*. We've since learned Khruschev meant we would bury ourselves with the same destruction as Sodom and Gomora described in the Bible.

Nearly fifty years later, I fear we may be proving Khruschev right. I pray our citizens and our leaders have the wisdom to recognize our downward spiral. Without awareness, there is no salvaging of our way of life. There is no hope against the enemy if it is inside us. ◆

Food Shouldn't Taste Good

Of all our "abuses," probably the most common is over eating. Recent statistics indicate that more than sixty percent of the adult American population is overweight. Coupled with a rising obesity rate among children, it is alarming.

When our nation was agrarian, people burned a high number of calories each day due to physical labor. Meals, of necessity, had to be big since so many calories were required to provide the energy for all the work. The end of our agrarian society, however, didn't eliminate the *habit* of big meals. The average American body no longer needs the calories for the energy but we continue to consume them regardless. Fat is how the human body stores calories it doesn't need for energy. Fat is stored energy.

> **Eating becomes, strange as it may sound, a deadly habit**

Dangerously, snack foods and junk foods have replaced big (and regularly scheduled) family meals. Many people find food a palliative for their troubles, and snack foods become convenient analgesics for their souls. Eating becomes, strange as it may sound, a deadly habit.

I see entire industries attempting to make low calorie food attractive and tasty. My experience is the better food *tastes*, the bigger the temptation to overeat.

I don't believe food was designed to taste good! If it didn't, I probably would never overeat. When cave people had to rip raw meat from bones, and chew it with teeth that were never brushed or examined by a dentist, eating was more work. Humans ate because they had to eat. If I were eating naturally, I would eat solely for the purpose of nourishing my body, not because it tastes good.

Recently, I learned of the high food value of sweet potatoes (yams). They are even better for you if you peel them and eat them raw as you would carrots. I did this and forced them down. No one else in the family will even consider eating something that tastes and looks that lifeless. The nourishment value of raw yams had no influence on their "sale-ability" in my home.

I also find it sad that a huge portion of our economy relies on "contributing to a national health crisis" for its very livelihood. Our country's best efforts at advertising are employed to get an already overweight society to eat more junk food.

In a newspaper article {*Grand Rapids Press 11/02*} I read that, "flavors release natural opiates in the brain suppressing feelings of fullness." I was happy to learn it is a physical fact that flavors encourage more eating by blocking the body's natural signal of fullness. If food didn't taste so good, few would overeat. We'd all be in better shape and our nation's biggest health problem would go away. I wonder what bad habit would take its place? ◆

The Power of Understanding

Shortly after my father died, I found my mother at home alone, crying. She and my father lived together for forty-seven years, and she was struggling big time with his absence. His death nearly drained her spirit. I thought this explained her tears; but I was wrong.

In her struggle to recover from the blow, she was out for a ride – to do a little shopping. Her trip was cut short because she spent a couple of extra seconds at a stoplight after it turned green. Speeding around her, a young man yelled out and called her an "old bitch." This did her in and she went home to cry. How helpless I felt as nothing I said could stop her tears.

> **Give 'em the benefit of the doubt.**
>
> Henry Schmidt

I doubt the young man (or anyone) would have said that to my mother had they known she had recently lost her husband of 47 years and was struggling to regain her spirit. I don't think anyone is that cruel.

Since that day, when I'm driving and I see someone in a car doing something I don't think makes sense, I remind myself, "Perhaps the driver just lost his or her spouse." I am not exactly sure why, but as soon as I say this to myself, I become more accepting of their driving. It no longer bothers me.

This has become my "template and lighthouse" for understanding other people. Not only is practicing understanding helpful to others, it also saves *me* a lot of frustration and disappointment. Coming to realize there may be perfectly acceptable reasons people behave as they do is a relief to me! Oh, the power in taking a few seconds to try to understand. ◆

So Much To Do Today

It is a sunny Sunday in October, and I have been planning this day for a couple of months. I am going to spend most of the day working on this book. I have had its rudiments on my computer for over three years and have failed to put together blocks of time to put it in publishable form.

When the morning broke, I was up early and off for morning coffee just in time to see the sun rise. Perfect, I thought to myself. However, it wasn't long after my coffee that it hit me. The *"it"* was the feeling of lethargy – the inability to get started on my appointed task for the day.

> **I have so much to do today, I'll need to spend another hour on my knees.**
> Martin Luther

I tried some of my established practices. I drove up to town and had a relaxing breakfast. I continued my avoidance techniques by driving out to our local airport and watching some planes land and take off. Guilt pervaded. Next I went into the airport terminal and pulled out my computer in an attempt to jumpstart myself. Didn't work. Finally it hit me. Some of the friendliest words I've ever read were at the top of the next chapter in my book. "I have so much to do today, I'll need to spend another hour on my knees."

"That's what I need, I said to myself." I closed my computer, sat down by a great big window and watched some more planes land and take off as my mind marinated in – well, in nothing! No, absolutely nothing! I recalled that I had just finished one of the most stressful weeks of my life making final arrangements for a construction loan that, for unnamed reasons, took more than three years.

"I'm mentally exhausted," I thought to myself and just sat for about a half hour. That is all it took for my mind to refresh. I re-opened my computer and easily wrote this chapter and several others. My day was a success, but only after I gave my mind and body an "hour on its knees."

Many of us in the United States of America are of Western European heritage. Our culture eliminated the afternoon siesta/shutdown that remains a mainstay in most of the "Old Country." Our forefathers who braved the trip across the ocean to the land of plenty replaced the siesta with the Protestant Work Ethic. They believed if you are not pushing a rock up a hill you're not working. I believe that's a lot of bunk! Since I came across the title of this chapter in my book/life, I need to remind myself regularly that, often, the best way to get something done is to drop everything and take a break, maybe even a nap.

If he were alive, I'd personally thank Martin Luther for confessing his secret to daily renewal. Spending an "hour on my knees" is so productive; so bottom-line effective. ◆

Enjoy The Moment

I grew up the son of a worrier. I would guess that somewhere between seventy and ninety percent of us (U.S. citizens) were raised by at least one parent who was a chronic worrier. I'm convinced a person *learns* to worry, usually from parents. This lifestyle flies in the face of *Good Advice*. Further, worrying robs us of the true substance of joy in our lives – the ability to appreciate and give thanks for all that we have at the moment.

> Worry: An un-
> healthy anticipation
> of your future.

Today happens to be one of those days that every-thing is going my way! It is sunny outside, I overcame an early morning lethargy that forecasted a wasted day in the accomplishment of this book, my family is all doing fine, my health is excellent and my future looks bright. We will be starting a new family home on a beautiful river site outside of town.

I need to take time, periodically, just to appreciate all of this. I try to overcome my worrying genetics and close out what foreboding circumstances may welcome me with a new day. I must face adversity if and when it unfolds. I mustn't anticipate it and busy my mind with it.

I accept the fact it takes an effort to enjoy the present. The present is the only moment guaranteed me. At any moment, the present may be my last moment so I need to be sure to enjoy each of them. My "last moment" will arrive someday. Until it does, I pray I will have spent the moment prior looking out a window on a sunny day giving thanks for everything with which God has blessed me. That is enjoying the *now*, the only moment I'm guaranteed.

If you are a worrier, know that worrying is but an unhealthy anticipation of your future. Ask yourself what reason you have to believe your future might be dim, especially since you can make so many choices to make it bright! ◆

Do Unto Others

The "Golden Rule," everyone knows, says, "Do unto others as you would have them do unto you." Seems to make sense, but I also think it is an example of how many of us have a tendency to know what is best for other people. We decide what we would like for ourselves then we set about (with all humanitarian intent) to do for the next person what we would want done for or given to ourselves.

> ... Another form of judgment - judgment that others are usually better off without!

Often our mistake is that what we want for ourselves is, at best, a distant cousin to what the other person wants or needs.

Allowing others to determine what they want and need for themselves affirms their abilities of self-determination and control. For me to determine what someone else needs or wants casts doubt on their ability to manage their own lives. It is a form of judgment and usually unwelcome.

Far too many of us carry the *liability* of judging what is good for other people based on what is good for *us*. Whatever mask we put on it, we need to recognize it for the villain it is: judgment. It's a subtle revelation of our belief that other people should be more like us.

Doing for others that which *they* would like done works for societies as well as next-door neighbors. Every individual, every race and every nation needs the pride of self-determination and self-control. Everyone needs to learn self-control and management.

The golden rule should be, "Do unto others as *they* would have you do unto them." This would help others in ways meaningful to them, not to us. ◆

The Masks I Wear
- don't be fooled

A popular song by Stevie Wonder contains the words, "No New Year's Day to celebrate, no candy covered hearts to give away." The singer is explaining that there is nothing special about the day, and that he is simply calling to say, "I love you" to someone special in his life.

Attending a basketball game in my hometown allowed me a perfect opportunity to view the principle of people and their needs, in living color. The visiting varsity players were sitting in the stands watching the junior varsity game when the third quarter of the game ended. It was time for them to begin their "ceremonial" walk to the locker room and ready themselves for the feature of the evening: their game.

They were excellent athletes and a good-looking group. They exuded confidence and determination as they walked. Along their route was a young man in his 20s, I'd guess, who sat in a wheel chair. He was from their town and it appeared as though he might have been paralyzed in an accident of some sort. As the ball players passed by his wheel chair, each, in turn, stopped to chat with him. They laughed and joked a bit and he responded in kind. His face was beaming – he was...somebody. There were others from their school in their path but they only paid attention to the handicapped man.

Why, I thought, does one have to be paralyzed or otherwise handicapped to get attention? My thoughts ventured to all of the kids in their high school who don't merit a second glance from any of them perhaps because they aren't "handicapped." At least, they don't *appear* handicapped.

When I began my career as a teacher, I listened to a man tell us of the power we had as teachers to affect children's lives. I didn't fully agree with him at the time but am in full accord with him now that I understand.

Some kids are overweight, unattractive, "zit" faced, abused, etc. But we don't tend to think of them as disadvantaged, handicapped or at risk. How much, I thought, could these basketball players do for hundreds of "handicapped" or "at risk" kids in their school? We *mistakenly* believe that most of them are okay and don't need attention because they *appear* to be okay.

I recall my experience in education as a parent, teacher, principal and deputy superintendent, and the thousands of children I've seen who were handicapped just as much as the young man in the wheel chair. They were psychologically, academically or socially handicapped. Sure, most of them had their physical survival needs met. However, their psychological needs to be understood, affirmed,

(Continued on next page)

validated and appreciated had not been fulfilled – ever. Their hurts were masked by their attempts to look okay and most of them were pretty good at it.

In a study done in the 1930s by H.M. Skeels (Hamer & Copeland), children who lived in an Iowa orphanage were considered mentally retarded. Some of them were placed with foster mothers who spent most of their time nurturing and caring for them. The resulting increase in the I.Q.s of these infants was dramatic. Most of them went on to graduate from high school and lead successful lives.

> We all need attention - all our lives

The foster mothers, it turned out, were mentally retarded themselves and living in institutions for their impairment. This proved that a child doesn't need to be raised by a brain surgeon to receive the love and attention necessary to become successful. What matters most is love and human contact. There are scores of similar studies showing the importance of human attention and affirmation. How much good each and every one of us could do for our future if we would simply begin paying simple attention to one another?

According to Maslow and others, psychological needs are second to our physical needs (food, safety, etc.). Second to food, people need to be understood, affirmed, validated and appreciated. Be careful that the *masks* I wear don't fool you into thinking I'm okay. Despite our outward appearance, without attention, nobody is okay. ◆

The Will To Love

I think there is a force that drives us. Work with me here as I call this force *love*.

"The will to extend oneself for the purpose of nurturing one's own and another's spiritual growth" is how Scott Peck defines love (Peck 1978). I like this definition because it frees me to use the word love with far more people than normal – and mean it. It allows me the use of the term regardless of gender or other social constraints. It lacks the traditional association with our emotional or romantic desires.

Imagine the good that could be done in the world if most people loved one another, not intimately, but with a simple desire to have an interest in helping the other person grow spiritually.

Notice that the definition highlights (first) "one's own" growth. The literature is filled with the idea that first one must love oneself before he/she can give love to another. I can't give something I don't have.

Many believe love is (or should be) effortless, something that just happens. We hearken back to the time many of us fell in love and can't recall any work to that. Where is the *will* or the effort in falling in love?

To begin, I agree with Peck when he says nobody *falls* in love. If we fell in love, then we would fall in love with our children or pets. Most people love their children and their pets, yet who can ever claim *falling* in love with either of them?

Just this morning, I awakened to a typical Michigan January morning. It was 10 degrees outside with a "ton" of snow. Being New Year's Day, I decided to take a leisurely drive to the local coffee shop and resolve to write a chapter in the book you're reading. As I got about ready to leave the house, my wife said, "I think I'll go and get a cup of cappuccino to bring back home." I said to her, "let me get it for you." She responded, "Oh, thank you, but that would be too much of a hassle. The detour on our road means you'd have to go out of your way and back home again. That's too much hassle."

I said, "True it's a hassle, but you'd have to get up, get dressed, get into an ice cold van and go through the same discomfort I would. Since I'm already going

(Continued on next page)

through that hassle, let me get it for you." She gratefully accepted my offer, my *effort* and my *will* to "love" her.

Love means effort. For me to love you, I need to extend myself. Many people don't love much (including themselves) because they lack the will, the willingness to put forth the effort. No effort, no love.

For me, viewing love as a willingness to put forth an effort to help another makes it simple for me to sincerely say, "I love you!" ◆

My Responsibility To The World
- bake a loaf of bread and change the world

I received a calendar for a gift that had a different bit of wisdom from the Dalai Lama each day. One of the days, the great leader wrote a message to *me*. It said, *"I have been to international bodies, I have been to the governmental and religious leaders of the world, I have gone to the leaders of China in my global appeal for my cause. Now, I ask you to help me free the people of Tibet from Chinese rule."* Dalai Lama asked *me* for help.

Strangely, I understood what I could do to help the people of Tibet. I believe I am simply a miniscule part of a gigantic thing called humanity. I believe we are all one, not separate and independent beings as our physical senses suggest. Since the Dalai Lama's appeal to me, I have learned of the plight of the people of Tibet. Simple awareness of their plight will help. I don't know how this is true, but it is, and, if I ever have the chance to do more, I will. I couldn't possibly help if I were not aware.

> **Every time you bake a loaf of bread you change the world.**

Most religions believe all humans are part of a larger being - we are all one in the spirit. All human beings are but single fibers of the fabric of humanity.

It would profit humanity if everyone believed that everything we do and think has some effect on everything else in the world. I'm convinced that what I do today, this minute, has an effect of some kind on the whole of humanity. This belief helps me feel a responsibility to keep my thoughts healthy and behave myself! It also helps me feel a bit of the pain and hardship of my fellow humans around the world. I used to carry Krishnamurti's words in my wallet to remind myself of my worldly responsibility. Here they are:

We are each one of us responsible for every war because of the aggressiveness of our own lives, because of our nationalism, our selfishness, our gods, our prejudices, our ideals, <u>all of which divide us</u>. And only when we realize, not intellectually, but actually, as actually as we would recognize that we are hungry or in pain, that you and I are responsible for all this existing chaos, for all the misery throughout the entire world, because we have contributed to it in our daily lives and are a part of this monstrous society with its wars, divisions, its ugliness, brutality and greed -- only then will we act.

In sharing these thoughts with you, I ask that you read them over and over until his message is etched indelibly in your mind. Do your part to teach our young the importance of their responsibility to the total of humanity. Their world will be better as a result. The "loaf of bread you bake" can and will change the world. ◆

No Football In Heaven
- the damage of competition

A friend prophetically announced, "My wife and I have a great relationship because we don't keep score!"

Another friend and I periodically conduct some version of a long-standing debate about competition and the question of its natural occurrence (or not) in humans. I argue it is *not* natural for humans to compete against one another. "There will be no football teams in heaven," is my way of arguing against the viciousness of competition and how, I believe, God doesn't approve of our growing desire to establish our supremacy over the next town, nation or individual. Because of its *unnatural* tenets, athletics usually brings out the worst in people instead of the best.

> When the One Great Scorer in the sky comes to put a score by your name, it won't matter if you won or lost but how you played the game.
> Grantland Rice

In his book, *No Contest*, Alfie Kohn (1994), provides researched evidence that, even in infancy, human beings will show signs of cooperating, helping and even feeling empathy for their fellow human beings. Babies in cribs, research has shown, will try to comfort and soothe one another.

I admit feeling a little un-American sometimes because I have come to believe that our capitalistic, materialistic lifestyle is counter to nature's idea of how humans were designed. Stephen Covey, in his book, *The Seven Habits of Highly Effective People,* (1989) describes "scarcity mentality" as a belief among some people that there are limited resources, rewards, recognitions and dollars available, and we need to fight, scratch and impede our neighbors to get as much as possible for ourselves.

It is more believable to me that it is natural for us to practice what Covey describes as an "abundance mentality" wherein we believe there are unlimited resources, rewards, recognitions and dollars available to everyone. It is in everyone's best interest to help one another get what we need. Helping others with what they need ensures that we will get what we need.

I observed some of competition's most ravaging effects while working in schools. Children continue to be pitted against one another for recognition, grades, scholarships, etc. in our academic arena. It's ill effects in the classroom are as easily observable as they are on the playing field. Time and again, college athletic programs are being placed on probation for recruiting violations. Recruiting violations is a fancy word for cheating; coaches will cheat to win. The same happens in the academic arena with some principals "fixing" test scores to

(Continued on next page)

make their schools "winners." Some years back, a major cheating scandal at one of our military academies found several cadets out the door. Even some of our brightest students are turning to cheating to avoid being termed "loser." Pitting one person against another in competition has the same effects wherever it is. It will cause some of the contestants to cheat. You see competition doesn't build character nearly as much as it *reveals* it.

I've always kept it to myself and some of you may be surprised to read that, if I had my way, we'd do away with all spelling bees and any other contests we purport as effective educational regimen. Contests are generally *unsound* educational practices.

It may sound contradictory that I continue to be an avid athlete and follower. However, the value I see in the competitive arena is quite different than the value most people see in it. The value of athletics lies in their ability to provide us with means to keep our minds and bodies in peak condition. Athletics can also teach those willing to learn that sacrificing their own selfish interests for the good of a larger cause will yield greater dividends for everyone. But this can be accomplished only if we firmly believe that athletics is a game – not our life, our self-esteem or our value, but a *game*. Very few people adopt this view.

Most believe athletics is merely a staging platform for "kicking the butts" of the next town's high school kids. This becomes their pride, their value. It is used as a means of heralding the superiority of "our kids" over your kids, our nation over your nation, or, quite simply, me over you. Beliefs like this are in contrast with the abundance mentality of helping one another to get what we all need.

I feel it is important to understand that *healthy* competition, does exist, but I'd guess fewer than one percent of people who compete or enjoy competition understand what it is. In short, healthy competition is basically self-competition – setting your own goals and working to meet them, not focusing on impeding another person from reaching his or hers.

The Bible suggests Jesus Christ was not a family {Lk 8:19} man. Families are another form of unit or "team" wherein there is more allegiance to an exclusive human group than to the universal truth of goodness to all humanity. Therefore, *extreme and exclusive* family allegiance stands in the way of universal peace for all people on earth. I share this belief, and it is probably as radical as any I hold.

Imagine labeling an American institution like family an "intrusion" on world harmony. It would probably take another book to fully explain this. I feel comfortable referring you to the Bible if you're looking for evidence.

(Continued on next page)

Good Advice

Broadly and generally speaking, there is only one team about which I feel strongly. It is the *team* of humanity. We're all on the team and no one was "picked first." We're all of equal value despite the *appearance of* differences (race, gender, physical characteristics). I've never minded the label of a "one world" idealist since I believe this is the only way there will ever be world peace. What Christian would argue that Christ himself was *not* a one-world, liberal idealist! He's the first one I can recall – a true bleeding heart liberal!

Competition between neighbors, high schools or nations will only lead to divisions, separations, exclusions and a host of other ills. I choose to search for ways of harmony and all-inclusive abundance, bounty and peace. ◆

We're All Prejudiced

I would like to share a couple true stories to help you understand my beliefs about prejudice.

I recall a newscast during the Gulf War (1991). An Iraqi soldier was captured and found to be wearing a Chicago Cubs T-shirt and a pair of dancing shoes. He explained that he was relieved to be captured by the U.S. soldiers telling them he was at a party dancing when some Iraqi soldiers captured him and pressed him into service as a soldier. It was an awakening to me because I had labeled all Iraqis as rather manic, emotional, chanting, irrational people who hated all Americans. I was prejudging them. It exposed my prejudice.

> **When you label me, you negate me.**
> Soren Kierkargaard

In the fall of 2000, I helped our sons change apartments in Chicago. In order to get into their new apartment, they had to wait for a group of four girls to move out. Having several items to move down three flights of stairs, including mattresses, chairs and bikes, I suggested that we help them out. It only took half an hour to move their things to their new place three blocks away. When finished, I commented to our youngest son that they were nice and seemed appreciative. He responded in one word, "hippies."

Steve, our son, is a great kid, and I know him well enough to know that whatever he thinks they were wouldn't hinder his caring about them or helping them. He is as accepting a person as I know. His "hippies" comment fired a tremendous curiosity in me, so I e-mailed him and asked him to list all the conclusions he felt confident drawing about these girls once he determined they were hippies. I wondered what he could say based on his prejudgment of them. This was his response:

"First of all let me clarify that the way you put it is that you said they were nice and I replied they were hippies, perhaps hinting they weren't decent people. I didn't mean they were not nice or decent, but you presented them as "nice" meaning possible dates. As far as that goes, I doubt I could date what I would call a hippie.

Now for the conclusions. I bet they are vegetarian, possibly vegan, feminists, don't like sports, likely weed smokers, have participated in some sort of protest (they could be major protesters or not) and are far left in their political thought. Okay none of these things are necessarily bad right? Well, in their essence, no, but my experience is that this group prides itself on rebellion and individualism, yet is as cliquey as a frat. A great number of their beliefs and practices are based on contradiction. They have a set of responses similar to a Pavlov dog whenever

(Continued on next page)

politics are discussed, and they quote material that they've never challenged or thought about for themselves. That's about the size of it. Love, Steve"

I was surprised at how many conclusions he'd drawn about them in the brief time we were around them, but it reminded me that I do the same thing, sometimes. I need to be vigilant for prejudgment creeping into my own thoughts. I am sure I am *not* alone in catching myself drawing as many conclusions about others as Steve did about hippies after merely looking at them.

Are we all prejudiced and simply don't realize it? Kierkergaard said, "When you label me, you negate me." If I label someone "mentally impaired," I am going to expect that person to perform only minimally and act a certain way. Early in life, we're taught to look at people, make instant judgments about them and expect them to act, be and believe in certain ways.

How they act (in our prejudgment) depends on how we've labeled them (Liberals, Catholics, Baptists, Jews, Northerners, New-Agers, Hippies, etc.) By the age of 15, most have a highly refined, unrecognizably deceptive system of "sight and sound" judgment that we rely on to choose our friends, workplaces, communities, etc.

At the least, our prejudgments foreclose on the possibility of forming new and lasting relationships with all kinds of people. They halt our searches for the good in other people. At the most, these prejudices contribute to the violence, chaos, hate and war that seem to plague our world.

Gandhi said we must become the changes we want to see in the world. I can do my part by monitoring my own prejudices. If I want the world to become less prejudiced, I must become so. I see this as my contribution to peace and harmony in our world. ◆

Every Child Is "Special Education"

I sometimes begin a section of one of my courses by asking the participants if they have children of their own. Most of them raise their hands. Then I ask them the question, "Does anyone have a child that they believe is *not* special?" No one ever raises his/her hand to this question.

I then ask them how many have children who are or were in "special" education? Very few hands go up. For their discussion, I pose the question, "If everyone has children who are special, why aren't all children given a special education?" Why are most children in regular education if they are special people?

> "Why are most children in *regular* education if they are *special* people?"

My experience tells me our best-educated teachers are special education teachers. They are schooled to make careful studies of an individual student's needs, interests, strengths, etc. From information gathered on the individual, a custom-tailored plan of study is implemented. This is ideal education. I wonder why it is that every child doesn't have the luxury of a "special" education.

Well over 80 percent of our children are offered *regular* education. The biggest victims of a regular system of education are the children who "appear" to be okay. They cause few problems, earn average grades and attract very little attention. One of the major roadblocks to helping children is that they appear to be doing okay. It's not easy to sense their needs.

However, in reality, their needs are real. Their needs for attention, affirmation and understanding are as real as the more visible needs of the special education students.

I believe it was Mark Twain who said there is no such thing as extraordinary people, but only ordinary people who do extraordinary things. I believe all the children in the world are special and capable of extraordinary things. To do a good job, schools should provide an education wherein each child is studied to determine needs, interests and strengths. From the information gathered, a plan of study should be implemented that is custom-tailored for the particular student.

Every child deserves a special education. ◆

The Spoiled Child's Burden
- The Best Lesson Of My Life

Approximately one and one half years after Henry and Marie Schmidt delivered their fifth daughter, they delivered into the world their first and only son, yours truly, Craig Henry Schmidt. To make it worse, approximately 17 years later, after attending nearly all of the home football games in their small home town (for years), Henry and Marie had the opportunity to sit in the stands and watch their one and only son play quarterback on the "Heights Tigers," *their* football team. Obviously, I was a spoiled kid.

Probably the most awakening and beneficial things in my life happened to me in somewhat rapid succession. They may have "saved" my life. If not, they definitely altered it and provided hope.

First, I had no offers to play football for a college. I couldn't imagine what was wrong with them. Maybe they didn't realize that I was the quarterback for the Heights Tigers. I couldn't come to grips with that.

> **The real world doesn't spoil you like your mother did. The real world kicks your butt!**
> C. Schmidt

The only college that had any interest in me as a football player was tiny Kalamazoo College in Kalamazoo, Michigan. I visited the coach and became excited about continuing my football career there. I was stunned when I received a letter a few weeks later. I don't recall exactly how it was stated, but it was clear that Kalamazoo College officials didn't believe I was smart enough to make it through their institution. My pride battered, I decided to go to a junior college in my hometown.

The following year, I went to Western Michigan University and tried out for its football team. Slam! I was cut from the team after a couple of days of tryouts. With only a little spirit left, I tried out for the ice hockey team and made it. I rationalized that hockey was always my sport – I should have realized that. While not a varsity sport, we played a full competitive schedule. I found my place and I decided to be a hockey player instead of a football player. We had a great team, I thought.

I want to tell you what an experience that was! We went all over the Midwest getting our butts thumped. I have not since felt so low, helpless, useless and – just plain *average* - as I did then.

This sequence of "body slams" turned out to be the best growth experience I ever had. I can recall sitting on the bench at Ohio University being mercilessly pummeled by the bobcats. With six fresh stitches in my upper lip, I stared

(Continued on next page)

off onto the ice surface and soothed my pain by saying to myself, "Am I ever glad I don't have to make a living doing this!" I also pledged to myself that, if I couldn't play this or any other game for fun, and fun only, then I wasn't going to play it anymore. This worked great, and I still play hockey with this pledge to myself.

It was a short four years, but a long, hard road from the gridiron of Muskegon Heights (MI) High School to the reality of life. I'm thankful for these years, however, as I can't imagine ever being able to face a world that doesn't spoil you without experiencing some head on "collisions with reality."

I post a sign in my university classroom that reads, "The real world doesn't spoil you like your mother did. The real world kicks your ass!" I'm surprised how many of my adult students agree and identify with this. I don't feel so lonely!

I work every day with people who were never *fortunate enough* to have learned this valuable lesson (or recognized its occurrence) the way I did. The best thing in the world for spoiled kids would be for them to have their butts kicked - mercilessly. While it happens often in the world (the kicker), it usually comes too late and isn't recognized by the "kickees."

I'm grateful my butt kicking came early and I was fortunate enough to draw the best lesson in my life from it. ◆

Nobody Sells Fuel Injectors

One afternoon, in a town outside Columbus, Ohio, I was walking through a small, recently refurbished churchyard. I began reading old headstones. On them were written things like, "Samantha Jones, 1810 – 1871, Mother, Wife, Friend. Earl Thompson, 1823 – 1892, Father, Town Physician, Friend, Church Deacon," etc. Each headstone summarized the contribution the person had made. None of the epitaphs boasted what someone had done for himself or herself.

I was in Columbus to teach a class. The following evening, at a local restaurant, there was a group of men in the dining room who were (noisily) celebrating the fact that one of them had sold more fuel injectors than anyone else in Central Ohio history.

> **What do you do?**

I wondered if any of those men would want their headstone to read someday, "Sold more fuel injectors than anyone in Central Ohio history." I came to the belief that when asked, "What do you do?" we tend to name some sort of trade. Actually, we are trading a talent for something else we need to live. Money is the return we normally receive for exercising the talents of our trade. The question is, "How do we use the money?"

DePaak Chopra said, "Life is meant to be joyous." Ultimately, most people spend their money to contribute to their joy. Picturing one of the fuel injectors this man sold, I concluded its destiny was to be purchased by an engine manufacturer who would install it in an engine that, in turn, would end up in an automobile.

The automobile would transport a family from Brainard, Minnesota to the Grand Canyon in Arizona. This journey to the Grand Canyon created joy for the family. You see, no one sells fuel injectors for a living. Instead, they contribute their talents that, in turn, contribute, however minimally, to someone's joy!

I interviewed a young man named Steve in 1998 and asked him the question, "How would you feel about dealing with all of the conflict in this job?" He responded by saying that, in the Bible, it says no matter what work one does it is all the work of God. He said, "No matter what I am doing in this job, I will be doing God's work. This will make the hassles of the job tolerable."

I believe whatever I am doing and whatever the fuel injector salesman is doing (know it or not), we are simply contributing, somehow, to God's work, the work of helping others. ◆

"Devaluing" Diversity

While I understand the intent of "valuing diversity," I've come to believe that highlighting and celebrating differences among us causes far more problems than it solves.

I witness many efforts to group people by certain characteristics (race, gender, location, religion, families, etc.). While well intentioned, this grouping interferes with the harmony it is intended to create and interferes with the causes about which groups are so passionate.

For example, where I teach in Phoenix, they have a class called, *Leadership for Women*. I wonder how leadership for women is different than leadership for men? I doubt it is, and I think it's counter productive to separate people by gender or anything else and pretend we're different. Grouping people divides them and slows cooperation and progress.

Forming exclusive groups tends to establish boundaries that contribute to various types of competition or contests between groups. This, I believe is at the core of global disharmony, violence and chaos.

I credit the *good intentions* of those who form groups of black people, female people, Polish people, Catholic people, etc., etc. It seems sensible that if we group together and exclude "unlike" people, we will contribute to the advancement of that group. I believe the opposite is true. I know in my life, whenever I feel excluded, I feel angry and hurt. Becoming more *inclusive* would eliminate a lot of anger and hurt in the world.

> I wonder how leadership for women is different from leadership for men?

Most people believe everyone has a spirit. In spirit, we are all the same. All the major religions of the world profess this concept. A universal recognition of spiritual unity would eliminate classes taught only to women or any other exclusive group. The rules are the same for everybody.

I've said before that Jesus Christ did not promote allegiance to exclusive groups, including family. I take a risk when I highlight this but when Jesus was informed that his mother and brothers were standing outside and wanted to see him He said {Lk 8:19}, "My mother and brothers are those who hear God's word and put it into practice." He didn't go out to see his mother and brothers until he'd finished his business inside. His teachings were allegiance to the family of humanity, not just the family that resides in the same house.

(Continued on next page)

My hope is that we move away from our practice of forming exclusive groups that highlight differences among us. I look forward to the day when everyone is expected and willing to adhere to the universal truths of time and humanity. These truths are not exclusive to any group, race, gender, location, etc.

I'm not sure of his exact words but Nelson Mandella said something to this effect: *As long as the color of a man's skin has anything more to do with how he is treated than the color of his eyes, there will be no peace in the world.* Mandella didn't specify *ill* or *malicious* treatment, he simply says, "how he is treated." I believe treating people preferentially or exclusively because of their skin color (gender, nationality, etc.) will create as much unrest and disharmony in the world as will such mistreatment.

Included in my beliefs are, "Affirmative Action Plans." Their premise is to give special advantage to exclusive groups of people. As long as we continue to *highlight* the differences among people, be they gender, race, location or whatever, we continue to stand in the way of human progress in a growingly multicultural world.

I doubt we'll ever see seminars offered in "Devaluing Diversity Training!" I think we could all use some because stereotyping, grouping, exclusion, etc. of people create anger, hurt, discord and violence – everywhere. ◆

The Shirt and Tie Illusion
The theory of The Origin of Unbelievable Decisions

Some time ago, there was a series of commercials on television for Holiday Inn Express. I thought they were hilarious. One depicted a tour group in a national park that was "frozen" as one of their group, a young girl, was paralyzed with fright because she was looking directly into the eyes of a huge grizzly bear. There was a man standing near her and, in an extremely confident tone, he quietly said something like, "Don't look the bear directly in the eye, don't show any fear, stand in a relaxed position and don't move a muscle."

> **People who wear necktics to work are smarter than I am.**
> Henry Schmidt

As the group watched, one of them quietly whispered to the instructor, "Are you a park ranger?" The confident young man responded, "No, but I stayed at a Holiday Inn Express last night."

The idea of the commercial was that only the brightest of people choose to sleep in Holiday Inn Express hotels, so he was ostensibly the most qualified to save the young girl. This was an illusion!

I developed what I call my "shirt and tie" theory. Before I explained my theory to my wife, she was confused by decisions made in "high places." Now, when a decision is made that seems to contradict logic, she will simply say to me, "Shirt and Tie!" I know exactly what she means.

Let me explain how I came to my complex theory of *The Origin of Unbelievable Decisions*. Perhaps it will help to clarify/dispel some of the disbeliefs in your life.

I grew up in a blue-collar family. Among other things, blue collar meant we were not smart people and, therefore, not rich people. So my father believed, anyway. Because I looked up to my father, I adopted his belief that the amount of money you had and your personal value were about the same: little money, little value.

Further, he led me to believe that men who went to work in a shirt and a necktie were not only rich, but they were smart. My dad wouldn't let me learn his trade (machinist) because he believed that machinists were not very smart and relegated to a life of poverty. In brief, I grew up thinking that people who wore necktics to work were smart people.

(Continued on next page)

I graduated from college and earned the right to wear a necktie to work. I was a teacher. While I never doubted my intelligence, I can say I didn't feel a bit smarter or "stupider" by wearing a tie. After five years of teaching, I became an assistant principal (administrator) and my tie became a more significant part of my uniform. As I was called to sit in administrative council meetings with other necktie wearers, it didn't take me long to discover that my father was way *off* in his belief!

Not everyone who wears a necktie is smart. In fact, many of the decisions made and conclusions reached by "neckties" reflected absolutely no measure of reason, sensibility or concern for other people.

I don't need to rely on fictitious television commercials to validate "shirt and tie." I can go to real life for a tragic illustration. In 1960, President Kennedy assembled what was probably as high-powered a group of "shirts and ties" one could imagine as his close advisory group. One of them was Kennedy's own brother, Bobby. To shorten the story, they put their heads together and came up with probably the greatest American "train wreck" in history (save, perhaps, the Vietnam War). I am talking about the Bay of Pigs invasion of Cuba. It was a disaster created by some of the "smartest" men America had to offer.

In the decades since this initial revelation, I have continued to wear a necktie to work and interact with others who dress accordingly. If anything, my experience with "necktie types" has revealed to me just how wise my blue-collar father actually was. I just wish he had known! ◆

Life Is An "Audible"

While I believe in plans, most long term planning I've done has been, largely, a waste of time. Let me share with you a story about legendary football coach, Vince Lombardi, as told by Don Mahoney in his book, *The Street Smart Manager* (Mahoney 1988).

Lombardi, coach of the world champion Green Bay Packers, said each year they would have an elaborate plan for the season that took hundreds of man-hours to complete. Also, every week, several hours were spent custom-designing the next *game* plan.

> **What you see "across the line of scrimmage" in your life will often look different than what you planned for in the huddle.**

Sometimes they even had a plan for the first half of the ballgame. In the actual game, when the Packers had the football, all eleven players would gather in a huddle and they would make a plan for the *particular play* to be run. Finally, the quarterback would get to the line of scrimmage, (to run the play) glance across the line at the opponent and see something unexpected – something they didn't know when they made the plan in the huddle.

This prompted the quarterback, at the last second, to bark out what is known in football circles as an "audible." In effect, he would change the plan right there on the spot. This is routine in football. Nearly all the hours invested in planning went down the drain in a split second.

Of course we must have plans in life. They provide us a *general* roadmap. Any planner or plan, however, must recognize that there will be thousands of "lines of scrimmage" in our lives. Without plans we would wander around aimlessly. As important, however, is the ability to take a quick and final scan across the line of scrimmage, and, if necessary, call an audible. Adapting to change in our lives is critical to our survival in a rapidly changing world.

What you see "across the line of scrimmage" in your life will often look different than what you planned for in the huddle. While carrying out plans, changing circumstances will destine them to failure if we are not capable of changing, or willing to change our plans.

It is important to determine what you would like to accomplish in your lifetime. Establish a general plan that includes a map to the end as well as means and resources. Plan on unforeseen circumstances and conditions. They won't change your general plan (goals if you wish), but they will cause you to find different means, resources and methods. You need to be "nimble."

(Continued on next page)

Corporations have come to *term* this adaptability, "flat" or "nimble." I emphasize, "term" because few corporations are flat or nimble. They are big ships that can't turn. Eventually this inability will sink their ship.

I'm not sure which famous general said, "No plan for war ever survived the opening shot!" I'm sure you could give far more examples than I of how your plans had to be set aside or altered on a moment's notice in order to accommodate conditions you had no idea were in the offing. Think of the last time you planned on a simple, relaxing evening at home and the doorbell rang!

It's healthy to come to recognize, accommodate and, most of all, accept that all of life, and every life, is full of audibles. ◆

When Will You Die?
- time is the critical ingredient

Dr. Jack Kevorkian is a physician who was vaulted to international infamy fighting the philosophical battle of honoring people's wish to choose their own death. Through some sort of process, people with terminal illnesses went to him to receive lethal injections. Included in the package was the delivery of their body to the morgue. This practice landed the doctor in prison. Courts have ruled, at least for now, that people lack the right to choose when and how they are going to die – at least with the assistance of a physician.

For years, I have been trying to find a suitable definition of "time" that doesn't contain the word, "time." This is a difficult task, but I did it. I define time as:

An opportunity to navigate this place in the universe, in this form, in order to fulfill a purpose.

In the part of our existence we call mortal we are all granted a certain (unknown) amount of time. To exist in this form and fail to take advantage of the time we have for the fulfillment of our purpose is tantamount to choosing to die!

> To me, wasting the time we are granted in this form is the same as choosing to die.

How many lives have we seen wasted by the choice of inaction? How many people spend their time on ignoble practices (crime) that run counter to the general welfare of our human race? I see these poor choices as choices to die. To me, wasting the time we are granted in this form (human) is the same as choosing to die. Time is the critical ingredient.

In the final days of my mother-in-law's life, she was on an aggressive treatment for cancer that was devastating to her body. In her last words to my wife and me she said, "This isn't living." I see the choice to die as different from the point that someone ceases to exist in human form. People can choose to die and still "appear" to be alive. Maybe Ben Franklin said it more clearly when he said, "Most people die when they're 25, they just don't bury them for another 25 to 30 years!"

I disagree that Dr. Kevorkian is guilty of murder because he provided people a dignified means to end their own existence. In the absence of a dignified means, people are left only with undignified means - suicide. I believe my mother-in-law chose to end her existence in this form once she concluded, "This isn't living." Giving up the will to live is choosing to cease this form of existence, the same as receiving a lethal injection from Kevorkian. I persist in using the term, "ceasing to exist in this form" and avoiding terms like death and dying because of my firm

(Continued on next page)

belief that life is eternal and human form is but a mere "parenthesis" in eternity. Death (as commonly defined) indicates finality and there is no finality to eternity.

How *long* I live is not nearly as important to me as how *well* I live. How long I live is one of the "gifts" granted me by a higher power and is largely genetic. The most I can do to influence how *long* I live is make good choices regarding my health and safety. How *well* I live is a choice I make and was also granted by the higher power. Failing to take advantage of this choice or wasting the time I was granted is tantamount to choosing to die, since all I have in this world is time.

Wasting time or using it for ignoble purposes (crime) is a form of death. ◆

Because I Don't Give A Damn
- can people be taught to care?

I want to share a true story with you about a chance meeting I had with an elderly gentleman at a McDonald's restaurant in my hometown in 1999.

On my way into the restaurant, I noticed a rather dapper man exiting. He wanted to talk so I listened to him. He told me he lived at the Olds Manor downtown. I knew that was a home for some of our poorer elderly, so I was surprised to see that he was driving a fairly nice Chevy Lumina.

> In order for you to get what you want and need in life, you need to help others get what they want and need.

He went on to tell me he would drive to various McDonalds restaurants in our area to stop for coffee and conversation with some of his regular buddies. He said the others at the Olds Manor were jealous because he had a car and could do that. I asked him why he didn't take a different fellow with him periodically. He answered me, "Because I don't give a damn." Stunned, I walked away asking myself (as I continue to do), "Can people be taught to care?"

I came to the conclusion that to teach someone to care, a vital element for good relationships, we'd have to get them to understand and accept "the law of reproduction." Many know of this law, but only precious few recognize it as a foundational element of forming and retaining good relationships.

The law states simply, "In order for you to get what you want and need in life, you need to help others get what they want and need." You need to give unselfishly and unconditionally. This will always yield positive and abundant results for you – it's a law! There are some important corollaries to this law:

1. You don't always get from the people to whom you give.

2. You don't always get back what you need – right away!

3. Accept that you do the giving and helping – first!

4. You can't expect to get something back. You need to give to and help others without expectation.

Giving of oneself in order to receive may sound selfish; it's not. The man at McDonalds doesn't realize he'd enjoy life more if he practiced the law of reproduction. He needed someone to listen to him. If I knew he practiced this law, I would have found it easier to give him my time by listening. Admittedly, knowing he didn't "give a damn" made it difficult for me.

While I question it often and have yet to conclude finally, I believe people can be taught to care. People can be taught the law of reproduction. I'd feel hopeless if I didn't believe this. ◆

"Discipline"

In my efforts to improve my life and character, the practice of *"discipline"* surfaces more than any other. Any improvement I seek or have ever sought requires some degree of discipline. Without question, the best means of discipline I've seen are M. Scott Peck's four *tools*: deferred gratification, acceptance of responsibility, dedication to truth and reality, and balancing (Peck 1978). I'll summarize them.

> **Mental health is an ongoing search for truth and reality - at any cost.**
> M. Scott Peck

1. *Delay Gratification*: Daniel Goleman, in his book, *Emotional Intelligence*, (1995) describes a study in which children were given an opportunity to eat a marshmallow right away or wait ten minutes and receive an additional marshmallow. It was a simple measure of a youngster's ability to defer his/her gratification. A longitudinal study of these youngsters found that the youngsters who were *unable* to defer their desires (control their impulse to eat the marshmallow) had a troubled psychological portrait. Social adjustment and relationship-forming ability was limited in these grab–the-marshmallow youngsters.

The opposite was true in the lives of the preschoolers who were able to control their impulse, to defer their gratification. The ability to set things or desires aside for the moment and invest in our future is foundational to a healthy, productive life. Most of the problems in our lives result from sacrificing what we want most for what we want now. It is our inability to stem our emotional desire to please ourselves in the moment that complicates and burdens our lives.

2. *Acceptance of Responsibility*: It's easy to spot those who are unwilling to accept responsibility for *their* actions because there are so many of them. They are the blamers among us who are constantly asking that we focus on circumstances and conditions in the world other than their behavior. They lack the self-security to admit that they are responsible for the way people (and the world) treat them. It is the world that is flawed, not them.

Peck labels this type of person *character disordered*. Another cornerstone of a rewarding life is accepting the appropriate amount of responsibility for everything that happens to you in your life. I emphasize appropriate amount because it is possible to accept too much responsibility for what happens. These are the neurotics among us who believe they are responsible for "everything" that happens to them and others. We need to balance the two. It is easier to treat a neurotic person than one who is character disordered. "Blamers" make disastrous parents because they teach their children to blame everybody and everything else for the conditions in their lives.

(Continued on next page)

3. *Dedication To The Truth*: Someone from Texas once said, "Lord, give me power to search for the truth and spare me the company of those who have already found it." Experience and history suggest there is very little considered universally and forever true. At one point in time, it was "true" that the earth was flat as well as the center of the universe. The "wisest" men said this was true and people were mocked and persecuted for suggesting otherwise. These "truths" as well as millions of others have failed to pass the test of time because of revelations of other "truths."

Peck describes mental health as, "an ongoing search for truth and reality – at any cost." A glance at our fringe groups, cults, far right or far left thinkers will quickly discover that, at *their* leadership, are people who have "found the truth." This kind of leadership searches for followers of their "truth." Maintaining an endless search for truth and reality at any cost is a healthy use of the resources God gave exclusively to humans. It is our duty since we are the only creatures we know who possess this ability.

None of our beliefs should be exempt from the light of scrutiny. Despite this, I believe a few universal truths exist among us. At this point, I believe the Ten Commandments are universal truths that have always been and always will be *largely* true. I have no interest in convincing anyone of my beliefs and I am willing to expose *any* of them to the light of scrutiny. Despite my strong belief in their veracity, I won't deny the possibility that *any* of the Ten Commandments could fall from its lofty perch of truth, as I remain ever vigilant for truth and reality – "at *any* cost."

4. *Balance*: I seem to have a natural tendency to do things to extreme or excess. For example, years ago, after downhill skiing twice, I ran out and spent a bunch of money to outfit my wife and myself with equipment. We not only couldn't afford this but, a short time later, we had our first child and I ended up trashing the same equipment thirty years later. It was still new!

I've done fairly well at learning to balance my desires and behaviors more toward moderation. I do the same with my beliefs. When I sense them getting too near the fringe or edge, I work on moderation. I try to enjoy the progressive value of the fringe without getting beyond it to the point of obsession, be it a set of skis or a belief about capital punishment. When a tire is out of balance, it needs to be adjusted or it will ruin other parts of an automobile, eventually incapacitating it. My own behavior and thoughts are no different than the tire on a car. Out of balance, they will "ruin my ride and me."

I've learned the value of these four tools of discipline in my life. Whenever I feel the ride becoming "thumpy," I usually smooth it out by applying one of these tools. This is close to the most important thing I know. ◆

Two Important Decisions

There is an old Indian proverb that states, "Every man has two decisions to make in his life: where you going and, who you going with; don't get them in the wrong order."

I don't know how many times I've been in groups, teams, councils, etc., wherein our task was to write a mission statement. A statement of where we were going.

I've reviewed many books about leadership, and have yet to find one that advises leaders to seek positions where the subordinates believe similarly to him or her – who are all "going to the same place." I realize this is rarely possible, because usually leadership or management is brought into a situation where they need to work with the people who are already there. On the contrary, when a head football coach is hired he is usually afforded the luxury of picking his assistants. He is allowed to choose people who are going where he intends "to go."

> **Where you going and who you going with?**

When I taught American History, I played a movie that was graphically morbid at one point. It showed the Communist Chinese Revolution of 1949. When the Communists seized power, they took the old Nationalist leaders and followers into the street and shot them in the back of the head. How cruel and unnecessary, I thought. I still think it was inhumane. But, clearly, the Communists had no hope that these people would ever do anything other than impede the efforts of the party to go where it intended "to go." There was no way, they believed, that these people would have a common vision or common mission – no matter how many three-day workshops they attended!

The single most important factor in producing a vision statement or mission statement, acceptable to the entire group, is select a group that generally wants "to go" to the same place. Millions of dollars are spent on mission statements because most people don't or won't understand this. ◆

Taker Or Giver?

In 1997, I heard Dr. Jane Goodall, say, "I can't help but believe that often the greatest *disadvantage* I have in my life is the fact that I was raised with what are usually seen as *advantages*."

I was showered with attention because I was the first and only son after five girls. While not a family of wealth by any stretch, I surely wasn't wanting for attention – attention that fosters value.

> "Anyone can overcome adversity. If you want to test a man's character, give him power."
> Abraham Lincoln

Having been raised like this tends to create the kind of person the world might classify as a taker. While I've always felt a strong desire to help those less fortunate than I, it has usually been balanced by a relatively selfish interest. As I age, I have had to consciously come to believe that God didn't put any of us on this earth to take; rather, he gives everyone an opportunity to navigate this earth to exercise the talents given them in order to *give back* to the future.

I heard that the environment on the earth isn't something that is given to us; rather, it is something that is loaned to us by our children. Any troubles I create in the world will be a sad legacy to future generations – burdens they'll have to carry.

In 1931, some of our ancestors made the decision to repatriate many Mexican Americans – send them back to Mexico so more "Americans" would have jobs during the Great Depression. Many of these "Mexicans," however, were natural born American citizens. Today, many Americans are facing the negative consequences of this terrible decision made by their ancestors. The current American population is repairing the damage done to the ancestors of the Mexicans who were sent back "home."

Chief Seattle said his people were taught to live in their lives planning seven generations ahead so as to be sure to leave their children a better world. I pray for guidance to make decisions that will not burden my own descendents, as well as all other descendents in the world.

I am here to give to the future, a future that doesn't belong to me, but one that is loaned to me by succeeding generations. This is a big responsibility. ◆

You Always Ask
- will you help me?

I am the middle school principal. At this very minute I finished a conversation with a pleasant-sounding mother. Today is National Prayer Day and she was experiencing a major mayday. She'd just talked with our transportation dispatcher wouldn't cooperate. The dispatcher wouldn't tell the bus drivers to allow the elementary school children to get off the busses five minutes early to gather around the flagpole and pray.

> **You always ask!**
> Phyllis Ryan

I put her on hold and called the dispatcher, whom I know and respect a great deal. Well, what I learned is that this mom had apparently committed a grievous error and didn't even realize it. The dispatcher told me the mom did call to *tell* her today was National Prayer Day and *demanded* she get on the radio right away and alert all the drivers to let all the kids off the bus five minutes early. The dispatcher said, "I'm not going to do that without orders from each building principal." Of course, this left the mom in a desperate panic so she called me.

Mom erred by waiting until the last minute. Therefore, she should have been humble. I have learned that when I find myself in a situation like this, it is best to "eat humble pie." She should have started her conversation with the dispatcher exactly like this, "I have a small problem and I need your help. Will you help me?" People generally want to help you out as long as it is something other than direct financial aid! I know the dispatcher well enough to bet she would have granted the woman the help she requested. I also know exactly *where* the dispatcher will tell most people to put their "demands." I know a lot of people like that. Always ask! ◆

Natural Or Man Made

On one of my many trips to Phoenix, Arizona I enjoyed a hike up the Superstition Mountains. I stopped, as I often do, to enjoy the scenery. As I gazed to the east, I saw beautiful, majestic mountains. Their beauty is awe inspiring, their size humbling. The absence of any man-made noise adds to the majesty. Gazing to the west I saw the "Sun Valley" of the Phoenix area. A hazy fog hung over the network of roadways and houses, all of which looked much the same from that altitude in the mountains. Phoenix was man made; the mountains and the sky were made by a higher power.

As I sat in the rocky desert, I watched a bird as it busily flew back and forth constructing a nest. I only watched her for a half hour but she must have worked all day on it. Later, on my way down the mountain, I took a break and, gazing downward, I noticed thousands of tiny ants going into and out of a hole in the ground. Those going in had something they were carrying; those going out were empty handed, off to pick up a new load.

> **"I just loved them and trusted them."**

Neither the bird nor the ants have the ability to think about their purpose on the earth, but it is crystal clear that they are accomplishing a purpose. Programmed into their DNA is a lifetime of orders that occupy their every waking moment – without a single thought.

These two observations (the mountains and the valley), and the bird and the ant working tirelessly without thinking about their purpose, led me to the idea that most of us think too hard about our purpose and don't just do what might be genetically programmed into our DNA.

I remember reading about a mother who had raised eight fine children, all of whom were successful. She was asked how she did it. Her response stays in my head. "I don't know, I just loved them and trusted them." It came to me that, like the mountains, nature is perfect and majestically beautiful – kind of simple. This mother didn't mention reading a seven hundred-page book on how to raise children; she just did what came natural by loving and trusting them.

Perhaps our blessing of being the only creature on the earth that can contemplate our purpose has handicapped our search for it. Perhaps we should be more like the mountains and less like the valley. Maybe we should just let go a bit and search for what comes naturally to us. ◆

The Story of Helen
- who's helping whom?

Our son, Steve, began a relationship with an elderly woman confined to a wheel chair in a rest home. Her name is Helen Eidson (pronounced Edson). He did this while in college at Kalamazoo, Michigan. When he left for a different university in Chicago, I maintained visits with Helen.

I admire this woman woman. In 1994, a stroke left her unable to walk but she manages to get around in her wheel chair. I imagine myself in a wheel chair and wonder if I could maintain her positive outlook. Many people in her position have a difficult time finding reasons to go on. Not Helen. I've often wondered what keeps her going. Talking with her provides the answer.

This woman is continually writing letters to friends. If there is a social cause she believes in, she writes. Once I found her in a letter writing campaign (mostly to the U.S. Postmaster) to get him to print a stamp with the Poinciana tree on it. She was on a mission to have this beauty recognized and shared with the entire United States.

> **I have nothing to complain about.**

Each time I visit, she continues to talk optimistically about what she needs to accomplish. I used to be sad when I saw her confinement but no longer. When she begins to talk with excitement in her voice, I feel stronger.

In 1999, I mentioned to her that I was going to write a book. She lit up like a fire with excitement. "I want a copy right away," she beamed. Her excitement about my book continues to inspire me to finish and publish it. She'll get the first copy.

I remember when our son phoned me with the news that Helen suffered a second, minor stroke. She was moved to a care facility where the cases were more severe. Steve went to visit her as soon as she arrived and found her sleeping, weak from her setback.

After awakening, Steve told her that his dad was teaching in Lima, Ohio and told his class about Helen Eidson. He told the students about her courage, optimism and determination to walk again despite her condition. Mustering all the energy she could to talk, Helen said to Steve, "Wait 'til they see what I do next!" We both cried over the phone.

More than a year later (following the second stroke), I stopped to visit Helen. She was writing to Senator Danforth telling him what an inspiration his grandfa-

(Continued on next page)

ther's book was to her. She is in her early eighties, confined to a wheel chair, and *she* is writing thank *him* for inspiring *her*. She has the tail wagging the dog!

People like Helen Eidson have an amazing will to live. She has a strong belief in her purpose on earth and uses every ounce of energy she has to fulfill it. When I see her enthusiasm, optimism and goodwill, I'm not only inspired but I'm reminded I have nothing to complain about. I need to keep busy changing the world, just as Helen Eidson does. ◆

Part of Problem or
Part of Solution

I once heard of a woman whose car was stalled at a stoplight. The light turned green but her car wouldn't move. Behind her in a big truck was a man who began honking his horn at the woman. After a couple of honks, the woman calmly got out of the car and approached him. As he leaned out the window in a frustrated pose, she said to him, "Ya know, my car won't start and I don't know much about cars. You being a man, you probably know a little more about how to start it. Tell you what, if you'll go up there and try to start my car, I'll sit in your truck and honk the horn!"

> We must be the change we wish to see in the world.
> Ghandi

I feel so good when I have a problem and go to someone and hear, "Let me see what I can do to help you." Even if they can't help me, I surely feel good if they offer. It even relieves my pain slightly if they say they feel badly for me.

On the opposite side of the coin are the people who have no interest in helping you at all. Much of the time, they are quick to point out your problem, as if you were blind to the fact that you're in such a mess or look disheveled that day. It seems that as you carry your heavy load, they find ways of tossing you another brick or two.

Below is the only poem I know by heart.

I saw them tearing a building down

A gang of men in a dusty town.

With a yo heave ho and a lusty yell

They swung a beam and a sidewall fell.

I asked the foreman if these men were as skilled

As the ones he would hire if he were to build.

Laughing he said, "Oh no indeed,

common labor is all I need.

For these men can tear down in a day or two

What skilled craftsmen have taken years to do.

(Continued on next page)

So I asked myself as I walked away

What role am I content to play.

Will I be a builder who builds with care

Measuring life with rule and square?

Or

Will I be a wrecker who walks around

Content with the role

Of just tearing down?

There are far too many "horn honkers" and "wreckers" in this world and too few "car starters" and "builders." Too many are quick to point out the problem, describe it, complain about it and wonder why someone doesn't do something. What we need are more people willing to keep their horns quiet and help get the car started.

The quote by Gandhi in the insert above is one of my favorites. I'm going to start today. It's the most I can do. ◆

Hearing the Wake Up Call

Listening is the most powerful interpersonal tool available to us, yet very few even know what good listening is. For sake of definition, a good listener is someone who keeps her/his mouth shut and is open and non-judgmental towards what the speaker is saying. A poor listener has little interest in what others have to say or, worse yet, feigns interest.

Last evening, I saw a poor listener become a good listener, almost instantly. I saw what it takes to get people evolving from a poor listener to a good listener – to heed a "wake up" call. I can find humor in it now, but, at the time, there was more fear than humor. I was in a meeting with a small group of people when one of the group (let me call him John) asked a question of his colleague (I'll call him, Pete). There were old wounds between the two, and John's question was a criticism in disguise.

> **A good listener is a person who keeps his mouth shut and listens.**

John is rarely interested in what anyone has to say to him, especially if it contradicts his view (see definition of poor listener above). Simply, the group sees John as a defensive person. He is definitely a poor listener.

Anyway, at John's question and, in less than a blink of an eye, a small female colleague and I were the only barriers between Pete, and John's neck! He was furious and as out of control as I have ever seen anyone. He was screaming at the top of his lungs with threats and disjointed stories of the past wounds he'd suffered from John. The threats sounded serious and his vocabulary would have shamed a sailor; definitely not something you'd want to repeat at a P.T.A. meeting!

I was too scared and filled with adrenaline to comprehend exactly what he was saying, but I was thankful for the little female as Pete had enough sense about him not to hit a woman. She was able to talk him down and convince him to leave. The meeting went on, but John was white and obviously not tuned in to the discussion. I understood why. There was a pervasive uneasiness that Pete might return with his rage.

I thought to myself how often I *felt* like Pete did. The burning, explosive feeling is easy to recognize and is usually a result of hurt. While few of us "go off" as he did, nearly all of us have *felt* just as angry. You see, anger is usually concealed *hurt*.

The next day, I was telling my wife about the incident and she simply said, "Sometimes that's what you have to do to get some people to listen."

(Continued on next page)

How prophetic, I thought. She's exactly right. This was the first time I ever saw John attentive when someone disagreed with him. It took a perceived threat on his very life to get him to listen

What happened to John is commonly termed a wake up call. I've had a few in my life. I'm better off if I can "sniff out" the signs before someone has to threaten my life to get my attention.

I know a woman whose husband left her a note saying he was done, gone. She was devastated and filled with question. To her friends, it was fairly clear why she was alone. Few of us would have stuck with her either. She either didn't or wouldn't see the signs forecasting the wake up call.

To varying degrees there are "Petes" in my life and yours. Sometimes they appear as a temporarily "wild man," and sometimes they are circumstances or consequences resulting from our own behavior. But, *they almost always appear for our own good to warn us.*

Our best defense against wake up calls is to listen to others open mindedly and non-defensively. This will eliminate the need for someone to "go ballistic" to get our attention. ◆

Ain't Gonna Die On That Hill
- the winning/losing disorder

I have witnessed hundreds of conflicts of various sorts and have seen scores of "contests of wills." Most of them are hopeless because of ego problems and a "winning/losing disorder." When two people have conflict and communication becomes emotional, a situation is created where there has to be a winner and a loser. In both minds, there is no room or tolerance. Losing is not an option; neither is compromise. So many contests are prolonged because they are between two people or sides, neither of which can tolerate a loss.

> **"I may die, but I win."**

I remember a basketball coach who had a sign above his door that read, "Losing is worse than death because you have to live with a loss." This is an emblematic statement for someone whose ego is so big that he is unable to tolerate (or live with) a loss. People like this are simply unable to "get over it," because their egos are so unhealthy. Despite *any* number of wins, coaches like this are disastrous to young people. Similarly, in many divorces, a wining/losing disorder has a devastating effect on children.

Most people in this state of mind masquerade their inability to lose by heralding the sweetness of victory. The truth is (this is important) that they are unable to *live with a loss* – losing is worse than death.

Sadly, this ego condition fuels many of the best athletes in the world, making them great on the field of play but huge losers off the field. To them, everything is a game "not to be lost." It is not only true on an athletic field, but in places where we may not expect to see it.

I heard a highly educated woman speak about a book she wrote. She had grown beyond the type of ego I'm describing. She told a story from her childhood. Once, when not getting her way with her mother, she refused to eat until her mother acquiesced to her wants. When her mother told her she'd die, she responded, "I may die, but I win!"

When two people with such egos conflict, communication between them is hopeless. Force or coercion is the only tool capable of getting either to relent. They'll cheat if necessary, because they must win (or must *not* lose).

I never took a Dale Carnegie course, but I'm told they promote a practice I've used for years. When I sense a conflict with someone whose ego won't tolerate a loss, I ask myself, "Can I live with the loss?" – can I accept the conditions of losing? If the answer is, yes, I will (somehow) express my willingness to "lose."

(Continued on next page)

Since the conditions of the loss are acceptable to me, however, I actually "win." The only thing I have sacrificed or lost is the need for my ego to be the winner. This becomes easier with practice and, believe me, I've had to practice it a lot in my life since I was an insufferable loser!

As a kid, I had a must-win ego, and I absorbed many of life's "beatings" because of it. Finally I became sick of the effort required to continue, "not losing." It wasn't worth it. I (painfully) came to the belief that this condition in my life stemmed from insecurity about my own worthiness. It is the core problem of many adults who persist in this painful existence. I now believe that, in many cases, being able to live with "losing" is the best avenue to "winning." I believe it is the best and only *healthy* avenue.

There are only a few issues for which I would fight to my death. Personal freedom and liberty for everyone is one of them. In nearly all other conflicts, I say, "Ain't gonna die on that hill!" ◆

You Gotta Believe

There are scores of stories emphasizing the importance of belief in self. Following is one of my favorites.

Tommy Lasorda was managing in the farm system, and he told the story of a team he had that lost six games in a row and, more devastatingly, lost hope. He knew that if the team dropped a seventh game, their season would, for all intents and purposes, be over. On the day of that next game, a story broke in the newspapers about sports writers who answered the question, "What is the greatest team in baseball history?" The writers determined it was the 1927 New York Yankees.

Later that night, Lasorda's team went on to lose the seventh game in a row. After the game, Tommy said to the dejected, hopeless bunch of young men that this was the saddest looking group he'd ever seen.

> Did anyone ever tell you the 1927 Yankees lost nine games in a row?

"Get your heads up!" he said to them. "Did any of you read the sports page this morning? Sports writers have determined that the 1927 New York Yankees was the greatest baseball team ever? Did anyone ever tell you the 1927 Yankee team, at one point in the season, lost nine games in a row?"

Lasorda's speech inspired his team and they began winning games. They went on to be the league champions. At the celebration, one of the veteran players and friend of Lasorda's approached the manager and said to him, "Are you sure that the 1927 Yankees lost nine games in a row?" "I have no idea," said Lasorda. "I didn't say they did. I simply asked the team if anyone ever told them that the 1927 Yankees lost nine games in a row. I was only one year old at the time. I just knew that I needed to get these guys some hope."

It was the team's belief in itself that allowed its best performance to surface. They had the capability; they lacked the belief. They could be compared to an internal combustion engine that had, "plenty of gas but no spark!" Metaphorically, their belief in themselves was the "spark" that caused their "gas" to explode into champions.

The same is true of you and me. While a strong self-belief won't allow you to accomplish *anything*, it will help you accomplish *everything* better than poor self-belief will. It is absolutely necessary if you ever expect to do your best at anything. Miracles have come about because of it.

You gotta believe!!! ◆

As We Thinketh

Given the choice, few would choose being out of shape over being fit. When we're pleased with our physical condition, we're happy.

To most people, "staying fit" means jogging, lifting, biking or other physical exercise routines. Author Covert Bailey, in his book, *Fit or Fat*, says, "Exercise cures everything." While I tend to believe Bailey, keeping ourselves physically fit is but one of four dimensions of health that is important if we are to be balanced and whole.

> Everything starts with a thought.

The most important component of health is wholesome thinking. *We* decide what thoughts are going to be on our mind; it is our choice. If our thoughts are healthy, our bodies will also be healthy. If I allow my thoughts to dwell in the negative, in worldly malice, and especially in the judgment of others, the damage will manifest itself in my body. While healthy, positive thoughts keep our minds at ease, negative, judgmental thoughts invade this mental ease, thereby causing .... dis-ease.

Negative thoughts make us sick!

The story is told of an old Cherokee who is telling his grandson about a fight that is going on inside him. He said it is between two wolves. One is evil, with anger, envy, sorrow, regret, greed, arrogance, self-pity, guilt, resentment, inferiority, lies, false pride, superiority and ego. The other is good with joy, peace, love, hope, serenity, humility, kindness, benevolence, empathy, generosity, truth, compassion and faith. The grandson asked his grandfather, "Which wolf wins this fight?" The old Cherokee replied, "The one I feed."

"Wolves" are fed by our thoughts. We choose our thoughts and wise choices are the foundation of good health. We choose which "wolves" are going to survive.

Another oft-neglected aspect of health is our spirit. Like thought, a spirit cannot be seen. It is our inner core, our unique identity. It is who we are. My belief in eternal life means my spirit is with me in this form of my life (humanity) but, being eternal, it existed before my conception and will also succeed this human form. A well-tended spirit, a contentment with who it is, will support physical and mental health.

(Continued on next page)

Finally, we are also social beings designed to care for and about one another. We learn best from others and we need one another. It is normal that some of us are more introverted than others. However, when we move toward the category of recluse, there is need for action. Moving toward the boundary of social isolation (by choice) often forecasts an imperiled mental state. Every human is born with certain "citizenship" responsibilities to the whole of humanity. Mental health is, to some degree, dependent on fulfilling our responsibility to our community. Humans have a need to be socially healthy and strong as we are social beings.

These four aspects (physical, psychological/thought, spiritual, social) weave together to create a fabric representing our health. The degree to which we maintain ourselves in these four areas dictates our overall fitness level. Chronic neglect in any of the areas will display itself bodily, somehow, as a disease.

My study and experience lead me to place primary importance on my thoughts. As DePaak Chopra says, "Everything starts with a thought." Thought is God's exclusive gift to human beings. The Christian Bible states, "As a man thinketh, so shall he become."

The simplest and best path to total health is healthy thinking, wholesome thoughts.

Everything begins with a thought. I choose my thoughts! ◆

The Most Important Thing I Know

In his book, *Dave Barry Turns Forty* (Barry 1999) Barry jests that the reason man runs into all of the aches, pains and minor surgeries in middle age and after is because, "He is only suppose to live to be thirty five years of age, even in the non-smoking section of the forest!"

I was fascinated to read a list of common characteristics of centenarians – people who had lived to be one hundred years or older. One characteristic on this list is that their weight has remained relatively constant (within ten pounds one way or the other) over their adult life. Recent statistics indicate that more than 65 percent of American adults are overweight. We eat too much. Finding comfort and celebration in eating, we eat more than the body needs for maintenance. Most of us overeaters would like to do otherwise; we lack the discipline. I suspect that people who have maintained a constant weight over 80-plus years of life practice good discipline. This discipline helps them in all aspects of their health as well.

> **We eat
> too
> much!**

I don't believe that maintaining a constant weight is one of the "secrets" to living a long life. I believe anyone who is able to maintain their weight has mastered control and restraint to the degree that they are able to say "no" to themselves when they are offered that extra "doughnut" (whatever form it takes) along life's pathway. They have the will to eat what they *need* as opposed to what they *want*.

I think it is this same ability (deferred gratification) that enables them to live within a budget, thus eliminating stresses on their minds and bodies that are known contributors to premature aging and death. It is this will and discipline that enables them to drink moderately (centenarian studies also show that most use alcohol moderately), work reasonable hours and generally live a balanced life.

I have my own vices and I struggle daily with desires for excess in various ways. I have always tended to do things to excess. In some areas I simply lack the will to do what I know is right for my mind and body. I strongly believe, for example, in the value of silent time and meditation. I have been unable to will myself to allot time in my day for this activity, as I flat out lack the discipline in that aspect of my life. I tend to "go" to excess. I lack a "pause" button.

Actually, whether I live to be fifty or one hundred and fifty matters very little since, when measured against eternity, the difference is miniscule and insignificant. Regular discipline of my thoughts, eating and exercise habits will yield a

(Continued on next page)

Good Advice

quality life no matter how long my body exists on earth. Therefore, becoming more disciplined is the most anyone can do to live to the fullest.

I once read a book titled, *"The Most Important Thing I Know."* It is a collection of various celebrities' responses to the question, "What is the most important thing you know?" Answering this question myself, I respond in two ways, spiritually and practically. *Spiritually*, the most important thing I know is that there is a higher power that, I believe, is thought, knowledge, and eternal. *Practically*, the most important thing I know is that living a balanced, peaceful, effective life requires the discipline to maintain healthy thoughts and actions. ◆

"The Force"

I was coming off a rough month, anticipating a return to work after a week's absence (I taught a stress management class). Missing five days of work put me further behind the eight ball than I cared to think. To help me relax, I decided to take a couple of hours and mow the grass. The therapeutic value of the riding mower did its job. By the time I was finished, I was up to tackling some of the paperwork that waited.

> God communicates through the heart

It didn't take much to convince me to take the work to our lakefront cottage. It's much more peaceful there and, of course, a trip to the cottage also held the promise of a little respite; I could picture myself sitting at the local bar, enjoying a beer and eating one of their juicy "Chicago dogs." If I was lucky, there would be a ball game on the television, and I could have two beers. Relishing that vision, I hooked up our wave runner (water toy) and headed off. It was 6:20 p.m.

Perfect!

About three miles into the trip, my cell phone rang. It was a friend of mine who I hadn't heard from in over a month. He asked how I was and, since he had the night off, did I want to golf nine holes? That was an easy decision for me. I don't particularly like golf - no, I don't like golf at all.

"No thanks," I told him. "I'm off to the cottage to catch up on a little work."

"Sounds great," he said. "You deserve a break. I just thought maybe you were free and would like to hit a few balls."

It was one of those situations in my life where, after three seconds of contemplation, I was overcome by the notion that all was not as it seemed with my friend. It 's a difficult sensation to describe but you've probably experienced it. Someone is talking to you but there is no voice or sound. A "voice" was definitely urging me to review my decision. I was still in phone conversation with my friend.

"On second thought, that sounds like a good idea. How about I meet you at the golf course in a half hour?"

On first impression, he seemed to be his jovial old self. Sure enough, though, it didn't take more than a gentle prod to get him to admit that he had experienced a career-related crisis and he needed someone with a "clear head" to help him sort it out.

(Continued on next page)

Good Advice

We went through the motions of the golf game, but our focus was on him and his trouble. Afterwards we went for a burger where he continued to unwrap his dilemma. He said he needed me at that time because he felt so alone. It was validating that, in his moment of crisis, he came to me for help. Who could know how much we both might have missed had I failed to listen to my heart when he phoned?

Some force beyond my power to describe, much less comprehend, told me to abort my mini-retreat and make for the golf course. I'm continually learning to recognize when my subconscious is trying to tell me something. It's talking to me all the time, and it's not that difficult to hear. It takes an awareness and recognition of its presence. When this happens, I believe it is God talking to us. God communicates through the heart. ◆

People Want To Help You
- but watch how you ask!

I am not sure if it was Carl Menenger or William James (both eminent psychologists) who was asked what advice he would give someone who said they were having a nervous breakdown. His "prescription" was, "go into the street and find the first person who needs help and get busy helping them out."

The power of this simple remedy lies in the fact that, despite what it seems in the current state of our world, human beings are designed to help one another. Just as it is impossible to eat crackers and whistle at the same time, it is impossible to help someone and be depressed at the same time. Accepting this fact can provide the cure so many people seek to the ills in their lives. I think helping one another is part of our human nature. We are social beings who like helping and need to help one another.

> **Helping one another is part of our human nature**

When I *need* help, it is a good idea to just ask for it. Since helping is natural, my request for help will often meet the need of someone else! However, be careful how you ask. When you request help, be sure to ask for what you need and keep it simple. Even though it may not be exactly what you asked for, accept whatever help you are offered - without criticism.

Late in 1999, I was helping our son move furniture from our house to his apartment in Chicago. It was hot and the work was distasteful and burdensome. My cell phone rang and I answered it. It was a pleasant sounding young woman who was employed by our schools but recently quit her job due to a disagreement with her boss. She hadn't received her paycheck and asked if I could help her.

I *wanted* to help her but, since it was Friday night, I asked her to call my office and leave me a voice mail. I would see what I could do for her when I returned to my office on Monday. She agreed and I went about my business. I felt good thinking it was my job to help employees, even late on a Friday night.

On Monday morning, I listened to the voice mail she left. Again, it was the pleasant voice reminding me of her request. *However*, her final sentence sounded threatening, "It's your choice, either get me my money or I turn it over to the Better Business Bureau." This tickled my "shadow side" (as Jung would call it) and deflated my will to help her. I hung up the phone and ended my involvement. I thought to myself, "The Better Business Bureau will take at least two weeks to help." I could have helped her that afternoon. She blew it!

(Continued on next page)

People generally want to help. A request for help will often yield more than asked. Be careful your request is genuine and leaves an option to deny your request without threat of reprisal or disappointment. Either of these can net you less than you want or, worse, more trouble.

It is important to understand that I need to learn to ask for and accept help myself. Since helping is natural, I need to grant this opportunity to people who want to help me. Further, I need to feel enough self security to admit that I, too, need help through the curves and over the speed bumps in my road of life. ◆

"God I Love These Guys"
- the motivational power of love

One of my favorite stories underscores love's capacity to foster cooperation. The details of the story have escaped me but the gist is as follows.

The board of directors at a steel plant in the Midwest wanted to find out why the absence rate was so high among their workers. They commissioned a management organization to study and report back hoping to learn how to stem this drain on productivity. A team of four or five highly trained experts spent a few days in the plant asking various questions of the supervisors, staff and workers. They studied statistics based on worker age, education, socio-economic status, gender, skin color, neighborhood, etc., etc.

> Anything of
> value can only
> be measured
> with the heart

During their inquisition they discovered one department in the plant where the attendance rate was unusually *high*, approaching ninety-seven percent. Curious, they visited the shop floor and asked to see the foreman. They were led to a large man who was helping one of his workers on a machine. Waiting patiently until he was finished, they approached him and sought his opinion on his workers' exceptional attendance record. Beaming and wiping his huge brow, the robustly rotund man declared, "God I love these guys."

Their research was nearly ended with the foreman's jubilant answer. Only one question remained in the minds of the experts, "How are we going to bill this company $25,000 and present a one-sentence conclusion.........God I love these guys!"

Especially in our country, millions of dollars and years of time are spent researching keys to human motivation. Most often, answers are found on the "shop floor," the last place we look. It rarely has anything to do with numbers or money.

As Helen Keller reminded us, anything of value can only be measured with the heart. I'm convinced that the foreman's capacity to maintain productivity in his little corner of a steel plant in Indiana was due to the fact that his love provided his men the affirmation, appreciation, validation, and understanding *everyone* needs - *every* day.

The simple truth is we must care about others and be willing to help them get what *they* want and need in order to get what *we* want and need. Genuinely loving (even the unlovable) may not be the only way to "increased attendance," but it is surely the simplest and most reliable. ◆

The Second Biggest Fault of Schools

I remember seventh grade when I, like all the boys, was required to take industrial arts. We were given a project that excited me. It was to cut out and solder together a watering can (complete with spout) for a Mother's Day gift. We had furnaces in the classroom and an old hand iron we heated to melt the solder.

I was especially enthused about the project when I discovered my father had an electric soldering iron – and an acid core solder! He shared my enthusiasm and worked with me cutting, re-cutting, re-shaping, refining, just like he did at his work at the shop. I also recall feeling excited about surprising my mother. It was perfect also that my dad and I spent time, not so much on the can but with one another. What a valuable lesson.

> Most teachers believe their value to the education of youth lies in the passage of content. This is the most common misconception and the second biggest fault in edcation today.

I couldn't wait to take the watering can to school and show it to my teacher, Mr. Cross (alias). I handed it in and it was returned to me a couple of days later with a "C" on it. My vocabulary was insufficiently mature for me to describe the feeling I had that moment, and I wouldn't include it in a "G - rated" book, anyway! Saying what was on my mind would have landed me in the principal's office.

Later in life, I learned that the feeling I had that day is called an "empty" one. Years later, in my studies of the research on effective teaching, I discovered what Mr. Cross failed to do was to recognize the value of the *process* of learning. Worse yet, he failed to reinforce in me the joy of learning and growing.

He was a wonderful man with no ill intentions – he simply did not know any better. Most teachers didn't *and still don't*. They believe their value to the education of youth lies in the passage of content. This is the most common misconception and the second biggest fault in schools today.

A feeling is created within us when we are excited about the process of learning (growing). *What* we happen to be learning (watering can construction, poetry, mathematics, whatever) pales in comparison to the fact we are experiencing the excitement of learning and growing. People love the learning process when, *and*

(Continued on next page)

only when, they make the choice of what and when to learn! I'm going to repeat this because it is so foundational to learning yet nearly universally misunderstood by educators. People love the learning process *when, and only when, they make the choice* of what and when to learn!

While there are some things everyone *must* learn (as you would drink distasteful medicine), most of what we learn in our lives is by our choice. Further, most of what we are *taught* in schools is insignificant to our well being at the time and for the rest of our lives. I am hopeful that, someday, children will be encouraged to learn to love the process of learning. This can only be accomplished by exposing children to areas in which *they choose* to grow.

Learning is a naturally rewarding experience. The best lessons of our lives never receive a formal "grade." In fact, nearly all of them take place outside the schoolhouse. Schools are not perfect. One of the imperfections receiving attention across our nation is the method we use to assess children. We have become comfortable with a grading system that was born in and based on the industrial era. It's outdated and, I believe, nearly useless at best and destructive at worst.

There is much question as to whether this system continues to meet the needs of our information-based society. As pointed out earlier, Helen Keller said, "The most important things we learn in life cannot be seen. They need to be felt in the heart." Test scores and grades are judgments on "what can be seen." Unfortunately, it is impossible to grade the most important thing we could do for children, which is to ignite an interest in the learning process.

You can help by simply understanding what I am suggesting and sharing it whenever you get the chance. Don't expect big change; you'll be disappointed. Understanding and sharing will help. ◆

Facing Difficulty

- the damage of easing pain by abusing alcohol and other palliatives

I have a difficult life and I assume yours is difficult. I assume that because I believe, "life is difficult." So says author, Scott Peck in his famous book, *The Road Less Traveled*, on the New York Times bestseller list for over thirteen years running. That is the bad news. The good news is once you accept the fact that life is difficult, life is no longer difficult. As I explained earlier, there are four practices or choices available to you – four "tools" of discipline. If I am able to employ these four, life's difficulties will be eased.

> More and more, our youth are taught to avoid, at all costs, the label, "loser."

In review, the tools are:

1. *Delay gratification* – Basically, this means I do my work first and I enjoy myself second.

2. *Acceptance of responsibility*. I am responsible for what happens to me. I try to avoid blaming anybody or anything for what happens to me in my life.

3. *Dedication to the truth* - This involves keeping an open mind, always being willing and open to examining my beliefs in case I might determine there is a different "truth."

4. *Balancing* - keeping everything in alignment and in the right amount. In other words, tool # 1 (deferred gratification) doesn't mean that I always enjoy myself *after* I work. Sometimes I might switch and enjoy myself before I work. So the fourth one is balancing the first three. The Greeks used to say "everything in moderation."

I've discovered that these are not easy principles to employ all the time, but the degree to which I am able to practice them seems to be the degree to which I am happy with myself. They seem to make the "pains" or the "difficulties" in my life much more tolerable. Unfortunately, there are also substances and habits available that will make the pain or difficulty *seemingly* go away more quickly.

Alcohol is but one of the substances or habits people use to alleviate the pain of their difficult lives. I believe the main reason people enjoy alcohol is that it creates a temporary euphoria, a release from the difficulties or pain they face. At least it *seems* they aren't as important or urgent. I say, "seems" because in reality their difficulties haven't gone away. This is not true only of alcohol. There are many other substances and habits that can make the difficulties seem to go away. Some examples are over working, over eating, gambling too much and over sleeping.

(Continued on next page)

The danger in overusing any of the "pain relievers" available to me is that I can become dependent upon them and, as I become dependent upon them, it takes *more* to make my pain go away. This is the point at which I become out of balance and the alcohol, over eating, over sleeping, over working (whatever) becomes but one more pain in my life. I've substituted a *harmful* substance or practice for the tools of discipline mentioned above. While difficult, even painful, the tools of discipline won't harm me like alcohol and other abusive substances or habits will.

The reason many teenagers try alcohol, I suppose, is mere experimentation. They are risk-takers just as I was (am). Being a risk-taker or experimenter is not bad. The difficulty arises when the feeling generated by the experimentation is such that one seeks to repeat it so much that it becomes excessive, out of balance. I fear our enchantment with competition also contributes to the problem of abuse.

Our increasingly competitive world places less and less value on simply being a *participant* in the game. Nearly sole emphasis and value is placed on *winning* the game. Most games produce one winner and several losers. Placing little or no value on anything other than winning creates a feeling of "loser" for all but the one winner. More and more, our youth are taught to avoid, at all costs, the label "loser." I don't know anyone who aspires to be a loser. Being a loser creates a pain that alcohol can *seem* to ease. This helps explain the rising use of alcohol among our teenagers.

There is also a social component to alcohol. Youth believe they gain acceptance if they are willing to take a drink of beer at a party. Refusing a drink may exclude one from the party – another chance to bear the label, "loser."

In summary, life is difficult. I face many difficulties each day in my life, you face many difficulties each day in your life and young children face many difficulties each day in their lives. Unlike unhealthy habits or abuses, discipline is refreshingly healthy and safe. ◆

Avoid Contests

My life is a little easier when I remember that there are people who enjoy contests. Research cited some years ago, by Selection Research Incorporated, suggests the enjoyment of contests plays a part in a healthy ego. "Healthy ego," is generous in my opinion because, in my life, those who want to make a contest out of everything are often a pain in the neck!

> **Never fight with a pig. You get all muddy and the pig enjoys it!**

Conflict resolution and decision-making have always been a part of my job in education. We are always trying to bring together a variety of thoughts, views and ideas and come to decisions that are good for kids in school. When we get a "contest lover" or two in the group, they seem more interested in being declared the winner than in searching for a solution that will be best for all. I imagine any organization experiences this.

I've developed some strategies that help me with personalities of this sort. If it is not that big of a battle, I let them win easily. If I disagree with a point they are making, I do so respectfully. "I see your point, but I'm not sure I agree with it" goes down easier than, "That's ridiculous!"

If I sense I am making no headway with them and I can't acquiesce to their view, I will explain I need more time to think about their view. If I want more time to think, I will say, "Help me to understand what you are saying."

Above all, the best posture I can offer for contentious, or any kind of personality, is to open up your mind and *want* to understand them. If one concept has served me well and remained true in my work over the years, it has been to listen to people and then, most importantly, do what I can to help them out. I find, even if we disagree, they will respect me if I try to understand and help them, first. This usually opens the door for them to try to understand and help me to solve the problem to mutual satisfaction.

Stay out of contests! Focus on your goals and work together to accomplish them without an interest in who is right or wrong. Understand that the need to win all the time or be better than someone else is usually the function of a person's ego. Often, they lack the self-security to accept the fact that they are not always the best or the winner. They're unable to overcome the need to be right and will work relentlessly to prove themselves so.

Never fight with a pig! Don't be lured into contests where you will get all muddy to the full pleasure of the pig! ◆

Behave Yourself

When I began *my* career in teaching, I believed the best way to secure good student behavior was to establish a bunch of rules for kids to obey. I would spend time each year going over my rules for the classroom as well as the consequences for violating each. It took me only three or four years to realize this process was a huge waste of time. I had about the same number of behavior problems as any other teacher.

> Misbehaving is always a choice and seems natural to the youth of the entire animal kngdom

I decided I would simplify and make just one classroom rule: "Behave Yourself." The kids liked this better and so did I. I was surprised to learn most children already knew how to behave. While some "Tomfoolery" continued, it wasn't because the students were unaware of my rule. They were choosing to break it!

Misbehaving is always a choice and seems natural to the youth of the entire animal kingdom. If you watch a mother lion and her cubs long enough, you'll see that the cubs' playfulness will eventually get to the mom and she'll "put her foot down" to restore order. They'll naturally break *her* rules.

It's just like life. There aren't a lot of rules I need to know to "behave myself." I was raised in the Christian church. In our Bible, we have the Ten Commandments. Most Christians can recite five or six of the ten! As I examine them, I conclude they are the higher power's way of saying, "Behave yourself!"

Like this message, most important lessons in life are simple and short. I like that. ◆

Make It Happen

For nearly fifteen years I worked in a position where I felt little appreciation and used few of my natural talents. I lamented about this periodically and, somewhat shamefully admit, I complained about it as if it was someone else's fault or responsibility. A little self-indulgence and self-pity obscured my vision of what I was doing. Now I accept responsibility for my condition.

I changed my life in 1996. I decided I wanted to do some teaching at the college level. I "buffed" myself up and applied to work for Communicate Institute and Development in Canton, Ohio. I was fortunate to experience a fair amount of acceptance and appreciation from the teachers who took my classes. I was gratified that I was serving a purpose in my life and the class content was designed to help people understand themselves better.

> The only difference between a rut and a grave is the depth of the hole

After two years of teaching in the Midwest, I began to think of my retirement which was only a few years off. I wanted to tie my retirement dream into another dream I've always had – to travel some as I do my work. This was the same time I needed to learn to search the internet, so I decided to spend an hour teaching myself to do this in the context of my desire to travel.

Since this was a search, I had to identify a topic. I wanted to establish some contacts in a warm climate for later in my career. I to decided to search for a college where water remained in fluid state all year long! I'd never been to Phoenix, Arizona but knew it was warm there in the winter. I typed two words into a search engine, "university," and "Phoenix." The first website on the list was the University of Phoenix in Phoenix, AZ.

I found that UoP had campuses in over 15 states, including Michigan, where I live. I made the appropriate contacts, completed my application process and became an adjunct professor. Next, I established communications with the Phoenix, AZ campus. It took me nearly a year and two personal visits, but finally I was able to offer my first class in Arizona in April of 1998. It was a huge success for the students and me. More followed and I continue to maintain a wonderful working relationship with the people there. It allows me to travel and fulfill my desire to teach at the same time.

I needed to take the initiative and the risk to teach in Arizona. If you are doing work that has you somewhat stagnant and you would like to rejuvenate

(Continued on next page)

your life, consider a risk. Ask yourself what you really enjoy doing and initiate an action toward work in that area. You will be amazed at how much is, and how many people are, out there that will help you meet your needs to feel appreciated and fulfilled.

You must initiate the action. *You* must take the risk. There are forces out there waiting to help but you must initiate the process. ◆

My Only Problem
- my thoughts!

Much has been written about the topic of thought. The Christian Bible (Jn 1:1) contains one of the more popular versions wherein it states, "In the beginning was the Word and the Word was with God, the Word was God." Later in John 14, it explains, "And the Word was made flesh and dwelt among us full of grace & truth." In a manner, John is saying that what you think (we think in *words*) becomes your body, your flesh. This is consistent with what DePaak Chopra says, in his book (Chopra 1993), "Ageless Body Timeless Mind. He describes, physiologically, how a thought becomes human flesh – how thought *becomes* the body.

> Everything begins with a thought.

The major difference between the human species and any other earthly organism is our ability to manipulate and otherwise control our thoughts. We have decision-making capability while other species appear merely to react to conditions and form habits of behavior. We are also the only known species that has the ability to synthesize thought – take knowledge of the past and plan for our future. We can contemplate, meditate, make choices, and so on, unlike any other being.

I believe most of my problems stem from my inability to align my thoughts with my actions. I am convinced that what you see of me, the physical, is largely a reflection of my thoughts and actions, which I control.

As an example, I know how to properly fuel my body, and I know almost exactly the amount and the kinds of foods to put in my mouth each day. I also know about how much exercise I need on a daily basis. As I sit down to eat, I *think* about what I am going to eat. I *act* by sitting down and eating. If my actions don't match up to my thoughts – if I eat more and differently than I think I should – the long-term effect is that my body will look a certain way. It will directly reflect my thoughts and actions. Again, thought and action are in my control.

The above reasoning is what leads me to believe there is only one kind of problem most people have – that is a problem with thought. Generally, the problem is a disconnect between our thoughts and our actions.

Most people who have a "problem with alcohol" *think* they should use alcohol in moderation, but they are unable to *act* what they think. When we hear people say they have an eating disorder, they work too much, they are compulsive exercisers, they are obsessive about cleanliness, etc., etc., they are mis-stating the problem. These, too, are all problems of thoughts not aligning with actions.

(Continued on next page)

It's worthy to clarify, however, that there are some who don't think there is anything wrong with drinking too much, eating too much, working too much, etc. Their actions reflect their thinking indeed, but this harmony of thought and action fails to protect them from the havoc that excesses wreak on the physical body.

Everyone has the ability to choose their thoughts and actions. Thought is powerful in its ability to direct and control our lives. Choosing to keep my thoughts positive, I will serve my total being. Everything begins with a thought and my one problem is controlling mine. ◆

You're Ordinary Only If You Believe It

My parents were not impoverished but considered themselves poor people. While not saying it directly, they intimated they were poor because they were not smart, and people who were not smart were poor. This contributed to my belief that I was incapable of writing a book. I can't say my schooling contributed to this belief but it did little to encourage me.

They *definitely* believed their children *were* smart, but their belief in me didn't transfer – because my reasoning told me that I couldn't be intelligent if they weren't intelligent. This was my earliest belief about myself. It took me over forty years to overcome this belief, but I have overcome it (see "The Shirt And Tie Theory").

I always knew I had tremendous talents in various areas but, like so many children, my strengths and interests were not the type to receive focus or recognition in school. This created my belief that I was an ordinary person, incapable of significant contributions. M Scott Peck (1978) convinced me I was an extremely competent person. I believe *you* are an extremely competent person. Periodically, I go to page seventy-five of his book and read the following:

....there is a vacuum of competence in the world which must be filled. In a world crying out in desperate need for competence, an extraordinarily competent and loving person can no more withhold his or her competence than such a person could deny food to a hungry infant. Spiritually evolved people, by virtue of their discipline, mastery and love, are people of extraordinary competence, and in their competence they are called on to serve the world, and in their love they answer the call. They are inevitably, therefore, people of great power, although the world may generally behold them as quite ordinary people, since more often than not they will exercise their power in quiet or even hidden ways. (p. 75)

I urge *you* to go back and read these words again, very carefully. I believe *you* may be an extraordinarily competent person and, especially with a vacuum of competence in the world, you have the responsibility to use this competence to make our world a better one.

I recall Twain's words that "there's a book in every life." I considered myself an ordinary to poor writer as writing didn't seem to be a natural strength. I believed there was a "book in my life," but I'd never be capable of writing it. Julia Cameron's book, *The Right to Write* (Cameron), refuted this. Her work convinced me that *everyone* is a writer – writing is simply talking with a pen.

(Continued on next page)

She encouraged me to simply write what I thought: "write to express, not to impress." How I wish more teachers understood *and believed in* the power of Cameron's wisdom.

Believing this, I began to write and write and write and edit and edit and edit. Writing, I discovered, is mostly taking the time. Late in my career, I began sharing my written thoughts with parents in a weekly newsletter. It came out every Thursday and aptly labeled, "Thursday Thoughts." I was overtaken by the response from parents. This inspired me. I now see myself as a good writer because I have done so much of it.

When I began teaching at the college level, I got a similar response from many of my students. They seemed interested in the lessons I had accumulated in my life and career. This served as a nagging reminder that I needed to complete my book. Despite holding a fulltime job and teaching for the University of Phoenix, I forced myself to finish my writing. I now believe I am as capable as anyone of writing something of widespread interest and value, and so are you!

I spent years trying to come up with a title for this book. In the five years on my computer, the document was titled, "Ordinary Schmuck." I had no idea what "Schmuck" meant but I learned it is a Yiddish term that can be considered derogatory, much like "bum" in the English language. Thinking further, I didn't like the term "ordinary, either, so I changed the title completely.

I am not ordinary at all! I'm convinced that the only thing limiting or preventing people from making extraordinary contributions is an absence of belief in their own ability.

There is no such thing as extraordinary people. There are only ordinary people doing extraordinary things. You're only ordinary if you believe you are.

The Indentured Servant
- and the pain of debt

I was having a business meeting/breakfast with an associate. He ordered the special: eggs, a selection of meat and hash brown potatoes. He told the waiter he would like eggs and ham but didn't want the potatoes. Mistakenly, the potatoes came anyway, a big portion. He ate every bit of the food.

> **Remember, Jesus Christ threw the "money changers" out of the temple.**

My study of emotions leads me to believe my friend was unable to leave the potatoes on the plate. He is a busy man in a stressful business. Like millions of us, he uses food as a palliative, an analgesic to the "pains" in his life.

Daily temptations surround us in a variety of forms. The advertising business plays on our weaknesses to the extent that I think we're going to see limits and constraints placed on the idea of profiting so much from human weakness. Every doughnut commercial, for example, seeks to profit on my propensity to eat junk food.

Like an unhealthy doughnut, consumer debt is currently the most aggressively marketed product in the United States. It is not unusual for me to receive ten offers for credit cards in my mailbox in a week. Unable to resist temptation to spend, millions of Americans are hopelessly mired in debt and filing for bankruptcy at alarming rates. We desperately try to maintain a lifestyle beyond what our income will support.

What do many of us do when we become hopelessly mired in debt? We eat too much, drink too much, work too much, worry too much, etc. We search for an appropriate analgesic for our pain – the pain of our debt.

I recall reading about "indentured servants" when I was in eighth grade history class. These were people who couldn't afford to come to America, so they agreed to work for a number of years when they got here in exchange for a ride over. In effect, they took on heavy debt. They were little less than "slaves" to the people who paid their fare to America.

I used to feel sorry for them until I realized this describes most of us. I find it discouraging that the best and the brightest minds are busy thinking of new advertising gimmicks and "psychological triggers" to entice us into burying ourselves in debt; into becoming slave to our desires. I believe we will see the day this "psychological tyranny" is illegal because of the damage it is doing to our national health.

(Continued on next page)

It's a sad fact of humanity, I'm afraid, that we are "wired" to surrender to temptation. Precious few of us are able to "leave the potatoes on the plate." We don't need any *help* from "money changers." Remember, Jesus Christ threw these very "money changers" out of the temple. He wasn't even polite to them when he did it.

Watch out for money changers lest you too become an indentured servant, a slave. ◆

Mostly Relationships

A teacher in Phoenix, Arizona shared the following story. He was having a difficult time getting one of his math students to turn in his work. He assumed the student hadn't finished it and wasn't going to. He struggled with leaving the student alone, and whatever he did seemed to have no effect.

One Monday, the negligent student came up to his teacher and asked him if he caught any fish over the weekend (he'd spotted his teacher fishing). This surprised the teacher and led to a lengthy conversation about fishing. Shortly after the talk, the young man produced several of the missing assignments the teacher had assumed he'd failed to complete.

> **Kids don't care how much you know unless they know how much you care.**

There isn't much to say about the story other than the idea that wise teachers will strike up conversations about fishing or anything else of interest to a particular student. The hidden ingredient in good teaching is *casual interest*, a sincere interest in *every* student. I call it "hidden" because many teachers don't realize this. Nothing works better. A good teacher understands, appreciates and, most importantly, utilizes the power of building positive relationships with *all* of his/her students - not just the likable ones!!

In my years as a principal and personnel director for a school system, I found the teachers who were critical of forming relationships with students were usually those who were *unable* to relate to them. They usually had trouble relating to their colleagues, too. Most teachers who form quality relationships with their students don't realize the value they (relationships) add to the learning process.

This message is purposely short. I urge you to read it again because this ability and *will* to form positive relationships is the most powerful interpersonal tool available – in the classroom, in the living room, the board room and anywhere else.

Should you find yourself struggling in a relationship, try talking about "fishing." ◆

When To Say, "Enough"
- when is living, "not living?"

On the news this morning, I heard there has been progress made in somehow reversing the aging of some cells in animals. I can't imagine where that will go, but the implication is that some day, when we get old, we can "get young" again.

A couple of days ago, I had a simple, half-hour surgical procedure that completely eliminated an annoying pain I had in my right thumb. What a relief that was for me. I was thinking that a hundred years ago, people probably didn't have this procedure available and they more or less "gutted it out" until they died. Well, people didn't live as long then as they do now, either!

The procedure on my thumb was the fourth "minor" one I have had since I've been middle aged. I refer again to humorist Dave Barry who quipped that the reason we need these procedures beginning in our middle age is that "Man is only designed to live thirty-five years, even in the non-smoking section of the forest." That struck me as hilarious at first but the more little aches and pains I incur, the less of a joke it becomes! I now seriously question how long we are designed to go on. When do we say, "Enough?"

> Man is only designed to live thirty-five years, even in the non-smoking section of the forest.

When my thumb was bothering me, it wasn't a huge pain. However, the constant little annoyance (on top of some of my other little aches and pains) helped me to see why, a hundred years ago, more people said, "enough" much sooner that we do today!

It wasn't a strong feeling, definitely not suicidal or anything like that, but there was a tinge of the feeling that helped me understand when people actually lose the will to go on living. It makes me thankful for modern medicine and makes me wonder just when people decide that it is their time to go.

I also referred earlier to the end of my-mother-in-law's mortality. She was a wonderful person who was suffering from terminal cancer. She battled valiantly for two years enduring the pain of the treatment. Her strong will to live kept her alive and able to handle the illness. On our last visit with her, she said to my wife and me, "This isn't living." Three days later she passed away. Because all of her efforts in life were focused on battling the pain, she decided it was *her time*, time to say, "enough."

Some of us will exit human form tragically and unexpectedly. Most will die of natural causes like my-mother-in-law. I wonder if all the little aches, pains and discomforts that seem to increase with age are gentle reminders that I need to be vigilant about recognizing *my time*. ◆

Don't Play The Kosters
- my best advice to coaches

I was reading a book about leadership lessons from General Ulysses S. Grant. One of his lessons was to respect the enemy, but if you hold him in awe, you cannot possibly defeat him. The Southern as well as the Northern press had sung the praises of General Robert E. Lee so much that Grant felt his own troops questioned his ability to face Lee's army of the East, despite his (Grant's) success in the Western theater of the war. Grant wrote:

"The natural disposition of most people is to clothe a commander of a large army whom they do not know, with almost superhuman abilities. A large part of the National (Union) army... and most of the press of the country, clothed General Lee with just such qualities, but I had known him personally, and knew that he was mortal; and it was just as well that I felt this."

> **Only give your opponent the respect you will give any opponent and never any more than you give yourself.**

As history shows, Grant's confidence in himself and the Union army was more than sufficient to overcome whatever handicap he may have yielded to R.E. Lee's superior military skills.

I grew up playing football and ice hockey, and it always seemed natural for me to be as aggressive as necessary when competing. I recall when facing what was purported to be the best opposition, I "up shifted" a couple of gears and put forth the effort to play the game. I don't recall thinking much about it – I just did it.

When our own children began playing soccer and I coached them, I recall how frustrating it was playing a rival team who had twin boys on it. These two were superior in size, strength and speed to nearly all the other children. I couldn't succeed in coaching our kids to attack these two aggressively. They seemed to get all psyched out prior to the game (starting to write their own obituary).

When the game started, our team stood around a lot as if to enjoy watching the superior play of these twin boys. I used to preach to them, "We're not playing the Kosters, we're playing soccer!"

One of my favorite experiences was when our daughter began to play soccer a couple of years later, and I coached her team also. Sure enough, there was one little boy in the league (co-ed league) of similar superiority to the Kosters (there is always one). Same story – I couldn't teach my team to go after this kid – they preferred to *watch* him.

(Continued on next page)

When we played his team and we were warming up, I gathered all of my little fifth graders into a huddle and pointed to the mini superstar at the other end as he warmed up. I said quietly to them, "see that kid, his name is Steven and he is very good. Watch him closely for a few minutes with me. Watch him carefully and study what he is doing." I paused, then, with my voice raising to a near shout, I said to the entire team, WHEN THE GAME STARTS, DON'T WATCH HIM – GO AFTER HIM AND GET THE BALL FROM HIM!!!" Even these eleven-year olds could find humor in the lesson. By the way, that worked great and we completely neutralized Steven for the entire game.

Only give your opponent the respect you would give any opponent, and never any more than you give yourself. If you do, the game is over early. In your life, make it a practice to focus on the challenge or task of the day. Never focus on what may be impediments to your success. Just understand their potential to impede your progress, then give your full focus and effort to what you *know how* to do. It is the only way to win the game or do your best at anything you attempt. ◆

Trust

I recall spending several hours discussing teamwork among colleagues. We concluded that our biggest obstacle was a lack of trust, so we spent several hours discussing means of increasing trust among us. It was difficult for me to participate in this discussion, because of what I believe must be done if I am to be *worthy* of trust, trustworthy.

> **Distrusting people are rarely trustworthy**

If I (or anyone) want to become a more trustworthy person, I need to commit to becoming a *better* person, period. It is nearly impossible to sit in a group and talk about becoming better people without the talk moving to examples of how some are "bad" people.

It took me years to figure it out, but I concluded that I have never seen a distrusting person I would consider trustworthy. Think about it. Many people simply lack trust in other people, generally. They see the world as a negative, punitive, competitive, untrustworthy, exclusive place. Their attitude is usually pessimistic.

I feel sad saying this, but there can be no group trust (at least total) as long as there are distrusting people in the group. Distrusting people are rarely trustworthy. Distrusting people need to work on themselves in order to become a contributing member of a group. They need to work to become better people. Usually they don't (probably won't) even see themselves as distrusting. This eliminates the possibility of improvement. I've dwelled enough on distrust and impediments to trust. What is trust?

Steven Covey (1993) believes trust is a combination of competence and character. The level of trust anyone can have in me is a function of the strength of my character and the level of skill I have to do my work. My character ensures (or fails to ensure) that I will be ethical and respectful of the rights of others. My competence ensures (or fails to ensure) that I am able to complete my work satisfactorily.

I like this concept, as I have seen some high-character people (nice people if you will) who lack skills to do their work. Worse, I have seen some highly competent people who lacked the ethics and sensitivity to the needs of others. Neither type is trustworthy.

I used to believe that my trust in someone was directly related to the interest they had in my welfare. I still believe this, but Covey convinced me that to trust them, I must also believe in their competence.

(Continued on next page)

Concerning my colleagues, the reasons for distrust varied. Most of them were competent, so the source of distrust in some stemmed mainly from their little interest in the welfare of or sensitivity to their teammates. This is where teams usually break down: character. The prevailing factor in weak character is a lack of concern for other people. I posit people learn to care by watching other people (especially their parents) practice caring.

I sincerely wish I could say we can teach or train people to care, but I don't believe it. I believe if children fail to observe adults caring about others, they can only acquire the ability if *they* decide it is rewarding or important to them. I continue to hope this is not true, but, at this point, I believe it is. You and I can only work to strengthen our own characters. Perhaps others will observe and admire our efforts, and this will help to encourage them.

To be trustworthy, I must care. ◆

The Dog By The Side Of The Road

Long ago, local minister named Duncan Littlefair shared one of my favorite stories. He told how he was driving to work one day and noticed a dead dog by the side of the road. He thought to himself someone should pick up the dog and take care of it.

The next day, the dog was still there and he thought, maybe a police officer should take care of the dog. Still another day, he thought maybe the highway department should take care of the dog. It wasn't until several days (and similar thoughts) that Duncan concluded *he* should take the responsibility to take care of the dog, and he did. This story is laden with meaning.

> ... simply because it is the right thing to do.

Recently, I was driving to meet a friend for lunch and was already a few minutes late. About a mile from the restaurant, I noticed a big piece of wood in the roadway. I steered around it thinking I was glad I saw it as it might have caused me an accident. I watched in my rear view mirror as a couple of cars behind me avoided it, too.

Next, I thought, "Gee, my wife takes this road home and it could cause her an accident." Then I felt good as I thought, "Yeah, *anybody's* wife could hit that log and ruin a tire or cause an accident." I pulled into a church parking lot, turned my car around and parked it safely in a nearby driveway. I picked up the log and tossed it into the brush where it could cause no harm.

The Chinese have an adage that declares a deed unnoticed is much more valuable than one that is. A good feeling came across me thinking that I had done a good deed and no one would notice. We should do good things just because we should; not so we get noticed. It has to do with moral development.

Thomas Likona (1994) has done a lot of research on the formation of morals in children. On the "ground floor" of moral development are those who do not obey many rules. Moving up the ladder are people who behave only to avoid negative consequences. Moving further up are those who behave or do good to receive credit, rewards or accolades. Finally, at the top of his moral development ladder are those who obey rules and do good by others simply because it is the right thing to do. Likona's moral development ladder is a beacon for me.

(Continued on next page)

I was happy picking up the log with no notice. It takes attention and effort to work up the ladder of moral development, but it is gratifying.

When I find myself saying, "Someone ought to do something about this," I begin the story in my mind, "Once there was this dead dog on the side of the road." This always tells me *who* should do something about it! Still can't say I always like the answer; after all, I am human! ◆

Who You Are
- and changing it

I worked several years in personnel and human relations. I couldn't guess how many hundreds of attempts I made to change people or get them to change their behaviors. It was late in my career of working mostly with schoolteachers that I discovered I was really asking people to change *who they were* - to change their personality.

Parker Palmer, in his book, *The Courage to Teach (Palmer)*, caused me to think along these lines when he concluded, "you teach who you are!" After reading Palmer, I believed I was rarely asking a teacher to change a technique or method. What I was really doing (most of the time) was asking them to change "who" they were or, worse yet, quit *being* "who" they were.

> You will be the same person five years from now that you are today except for the people you meet and the books you read.

At the time, this attitude is what created most of my frustration, because precious few of us ever change *who* we are. Maybe *who* we are is *what* we are. It used to be popular to say, "You are what you eat." Some actually believed it because there was a famous book by that title that stressed the importance of a good diet.

My belief is that we are what we *do* – everyday. We are identified by our *actions* and behavior over time. It is our actions by which we are judged. This made searching for employees (teachers) very difficult since, in most cases, I had little knowledge of their actions thereto.

Just as it is unwise to shop by price tag alone, I learned to first shop for the person *then* for their price. Experienced employers "buy the person" before they buy the product. The right person is priceless and if I found him or her, I'd accomplished well over ninety percent of the mission. Most candidates tried to show me their best side in an interview and obscure that which I would find to interfere with getting along with children and fellow staff.

In my early years as an assistant principal, our school focused on teaching teamwork to the kids. Most of the teachers worked in teams of two or three. While a team on paper, some of the teachers almost refused to work together. As an example, we had collapsible walls between classrooms and some teachers refused to collapse them and allow the kids to *see* them working as a team. Because they didn't get along with each other, they hardly moved the wall. As principal, I tried insisting they collapse the wall and work together once a week. This was tantamount to asking them to like one another!

(Continued on next page)

I discovered these teachers also had walls up in their lives. There were walls between themselves and neighbors, family and, generally, other people. They weren't refusing to take down a wall in their classroom, they were refusing to take down the walls in their lives; they refused to change *who* they were. The principal could *order* the walls down in the school but not the walls in their lives. They refused to change *who* they were.

Changing our personality first requires an awareness of who we are. Once aware, what we dislike about ourselves must be so distasteful that we say, "I must change." Wanting to change, believing we can change and thinking we want to change won't work. We have to say, "I *must* change" before it can happen.

Even after awareness and the "must change" epiphany, the process of changing *who* we are is difficult because we will have to change our habits (repeated actions or behaviors). If you want to get an idea of how much discomfort you will experience changing a habit, try wearing your watch on the opposite wrist or eating with the opposite hand for a couple of weeks. It is uncomfortable.

Imagine the discomfort you're going to experience if you decide to substitute jogging for watching television, reading a book instead of (ready for this?) sleeping an extra hour in the morning! This discomfort explains our reluctance to change *who* we are. However, believe me, the rewards of change far outweigh the efforts.

I heard Og Mandino say you will be the same person five years from now that you are today except for the people you meet and the books you read. I am not the same person I was five or 15 years ago. Accepting the fact I was in control of my life and taking action (reading and meeting) made me a new person. It requires daily maintenance but it is worth every minute of sacrifice. My hope for you is, if you seek a similar transformation, you will find the strength and courage to do it. ◆

The Gift Of Giving

As an assignment in a seventh grade class, our then twelve-year-old son, Steve, had to do something nice for someone and expect nothing in return. He chose his eight-year-old sister, Ann E. He decided, without prompting or threat of sanction, to clean up her bedroom. Well, let me tell you, Ann E. found his generosity most confusing. There was never a mutual interest in cleaning up after one another. This required coercion or threat!

> **What's in it for me?**

I recall how hilarious Ann's confusion was, although I hid my reaction to observe the "plot" through its natural flow. She followed him around her room asking him why he was doing this. "Is mom mad at you?" she asked. Steve went stoically about his assignment offering no explanation other than it is something he felt like doing.

Realizing she wasn't going to get an understandable answer, Ann E. pulled out her change jar, dumped some into her little hand and almost pleaded, "Here, Stevie, take some of my money!" This almost threw me over the edge as I eased away from the drama. I don't recall how it ended. The lesson, of course, was along the lines of the message:

"One of the measures of a true person is they give to people who can give them absolutely nothing in return."

It *seems* natural to give to others only for a reason, expecting something in return. Our way of life seems to encourage doing things for profit, not for people! I believe this contradicts our natural design. If it were natural to do things only for personal gain, how would anyone ever feel satisfaction by giving with no expectation of return? And many people do.

A refinement of this gesture is doing something nice for someone without his or her awareness that you did it. Bending down to pick up a piece of glass on a sidewalk, or remove a nail from a driveway so someone won't be injured, requires an effort that will usually go completely unnoticed. Simply doing good has a natural reward, also.

I can only imagine the difference in the world if but half of us lived and experienced the "law" of giving. ◆

It's Good For You

I'm sitting in a council meeting as I write this little slice of Good Advice. One of my colleagues is going on and on as if the rest of us have an interest in what she's saying. I chuckle to myself as I think, "She's confusing me with someone who gives a rip!" Humor makes her prattle palatable.

I'm sure I've done (and do) this *myself*. How often I find myself deciding what someone else needs to hear or what's good for him/her. It's not just at council meetings; it's everywhere, especially in our schools. In classrooms, there is a clear message communicated, "Listen up kids, I'm the teacher, I know what's good for you and I'm going to share it with you so *you'll* know what's good for you."

> **She's confusing me with someone who gives a rip!**

We follow the message by holding children responsible for learning "what's good for them." We test them to be sure they learned "what's good for them." I don't want to be misunderstood. I believe certain knowledge is necessary for anyone to become a responsible, productive citizen, but it is very little.

I think it's more important, however, to recognize and help students with what *they* think is good for them and what *they* want to learn. I appreciate people looking out for my interests (what *they* think is good for me or I need to know), but I would rather they consider what I want or need to know before they decide to occupy 20 minutes of my time or years of my life.

I can think of instances where people would have taken an hour of my time (had I not politely interrupted them) spewing information that I already had or didn't need. *They* determined I need to hear it and kept on talking.

People seem to appreciate me more since I learned to run things by them briefly before elaborating. Frequently, I will say to someone, "Ask *me* a question." This tells me what information they need from me. I wish everybody would do this before they begin rambling on about what's good for me! ◆

Average
- what we become and the story of Gordie Nickels

Teachers have tremendous power. There is a saying that goes something like, "We don't become what we think we are. We don't become what others think we are. We become what *we think* others think we are."

It took me a while to come to believe this. Other peoples' expectation of us has a huge effect on what we become. In my educational career, I came to respect scores of people. One was an elementary principal named Gordie Nickels. Below is a story he shared with me that requires no further comment. Its message is titanic for teachers and parents.

In the second grade, my father was among the parents who visited the class to see the learning process in action. I was called to the board to do a math problem, maybe seven take away five or something like that. I wrote the wrong answer down and the teacher came to the board and put a big check mark through it. I didn't want to look at my father. I hoped he wouldn't bring it up. My father was my hero and I never wanted to disappoint him – not even in the second grade. This is an example of why I grew up thinking I was dumb. In the seventh grade, I recall my father telling me, "Just pass the seventh grade. That's all I ask."

> **We become what *we think others* think we are.**

To this day I am deathly afraid to sing in front of other people despite the fact that I love to sing. When I was in fourth grade, a bunch of us went to the front of the room to sing four lines of a song. We were auditioning for a part in a play. I might have been the fifth kid to sing. Everyone who went before me sang all four lines, was thanked and sat down. When it came my turn, I began to sing but, after the second line, the teacher told me I could stop now and sit down. Everyone was allowed to sing four lines except me. I think this is why I still won't sing in front of others.

All through high school, I did just average and was satisfied because I thought I was average. I wanted to go to college and be a teacher. On entering college, an advisor told me something that scared me. He told me that, in college, I could figure on taking my high school grade point average and drop it one point. Well, my high school grade point average was such that a drop by one wouldn't get me through college. That scared me. The short of it – I graduated in the top ten of my college class at Western Michigan University.

(Continued on next page)

I always wanted to become a teacher because my father was an educator and I admired him so much for his wisdom. Equally, I wanted to become a teacher so that I could do all I could to eliminate the hurt that I felt as a young student – all of the feelings of being a dumb person.

I want to leave the following poem with you as it does a nice job of expressing what so many children carry around with them – forever. You can do something to change this devastating belief in children. When you've finished it, please go back and read the opening paragraph of this chapter.

AVERAGE

I don't cause teachers trouble
My grades have been OK
I listen in my classes
And I'm in school every day

My teachers say I'm average
My parents think so too
I wish I didn't know that
Cause there's lots I'd like to do

I'd like to build a rocket
I've a book that tells you how
And start a stamp collection
Well, no use in trying now

Cause since I found I'm average
I'm just smart enough to see
It means there's nothing special
That I should expect of me

(Continued on next page)

Nobody ever sees me
Because I'm in between
Those two standard deviations
On each side of the mean

I'm part of the majority
That 'hump' part of the bell
Who spends his life unnoticed
In an 'average' kind of hell

Author Unknown ◆

I'll Be Okay

Recently, my wife and I began building a new house. The start of the house represented a culmination of three years of headaches, financial loss, sleepless nights, disillusionment, ego busting and general disgust. A book could be written about the lessons we learned. What I hope to communicate here is a valuable mental analgesic (pain reliever) and stress management tool I cultivated as a result of this near "train wreck" in our lives.

The purchase of our land, selection of a builder and development of a house plan was headache enough but, soon after we dug the hole for our new house, one more twist in the road came. We were informed our house plan did not meet the neighborhood specifications. It was too small.

There are many details, but suffice it to say we were going to have to endure some "pain" in order to build on our site. For over a month, we didn't know if we would be able to finish building the house we planned. Thankfully, I'd learned to deal with my worry. I never had a worry in the world about the outcome because I learned to divert my focus from the "small problems" in my life, which this one was.

> Everything is always okay in the end. If it's not, then it's not the end.

Looking back on my life, despite its struggles, I conclude that it's been a great life. I have what I need and I'm happy. I can think of no rational reason to believe the rest of my life won't turn out exactly the same – including this "small problem" with the house plans.

I didn't know what the outcome would be, of course, but I believed that it would be okay. My rationale, again, was that so far I've faced hundreds of these "speed bumps in the road of life" and, despite this, my life has been great. I predict the rest of my life will be similar.

I use the term "rational reason" on purpose. When I worry, I am usually fretting over "irrational" fears. They have no basis in fact. If my life were awful, then I would have rational reason to believe that the rest of it would be awful. Since this is not the case, worrying about the rest of my life is irrational.

I was sipping coffee one morning at a small restaurant in Chicago right below some train tracks and this rational conclusion permitted me to sit quietly, alone. I knew my concerns would cease.

Believing everything is going to be okay is a great tool for managing stress since so much of our stress comes from worry about our future. If you tend to

(Continued on next page)

worry or fret a lot, I urge you to take an inventory of your life to date. Has it been okay? If so, what rational reason do you have to believe that the rest of your life won't be similar? If your life to date has not been okay, my offering of hope is to accept the fact that *you control your life*. You are in control; you can design your own future.

"No one can rewrite his/her past but anyone can write his/her own future – everyday." ◆

Do You Know What You See or See What You Know?

I enjoy telling myself a favorite joke and laughing out loud. Of course I do this when I am alone, usually in the car. I appreciate my ability to tell a story and I validate myself with laughter. Such was the case a few minutes ago as I drove to a mall in Phoenix, Arizona.

I told myself the story of the two farmers who had horses that they saw as identical. One of the farmers was tired of this so he cut the mane off his horse and took it over to show his friend with the exact same (looking) horse. To both of their dismay, the other farmer had done the same thing an hour earlier, shearing *his* horse's mane. The horses still looked exactly the same.

> You'll see it when
> you believe it.

Next day, the same farmer decided to trim twelve inches from the hair of *his* horses' tail. Parading it over to the other farmer's house to show him, they met one another about half way as his friend was coming to show that he had solved their problem by cutting; yup, you guessed it, exactly one foot of hair off his horse's tail. Their problem remained. They could not tell their horses apart. One or two more failed attempts like these and the farmers decided to measure their horses. They were jubilant when they found out that the black horse was six inches taller than the white one!!!

Abraham Joshua Heschel cautioned us that we should condition ourselves to know what we *see* rather than to *see* what we know. Wayne Dyer authored a book titled, *You'll See It When You Believe It* that describes how we tend to believe only what we already know because that's all we *see* when we look.

The two agrarian friends suffered from a "disability" that we all suffer from every day. They kept seeing what they were looking *for* and not seeing what they were looking *at*.

Ten minutes ago, I left a department store. After arriving in Phoenix I discovered I had forgotten to pack socks for the trip. I went into the store and found the men's department and a huge rack of socks. I narrowed my search to two packs of socks that looked exactly the same except one was priced at $ 5.34 for a package and the other was priced at $7.14. I looked again because I thought for sure one had two pair and the other had three. Not so. I checked again, and still not so.

I picked up each package and looked at the color of the socks and they were exactly the same, one blue pair and one black pair. I looked again, same thing. I looked at the materials in one package of the socks. It read, "ninety percent cot-

(Continued on next page)

ton, ten percent polyester." I looked at the other package, same thing – "ninety percent cotton, ten percent polyester." I checked each of the above criteria three or four times before I asked an employee for help. He was a stocker, a retired gentleman who said, "I can't help you, I'm only a stock clerk." However, he was a nice man and he decided to try his skills.

He picked up both packs of socks and said, "It's probably because one pair is our house brand and the other pack is a nationally-advertised brand. I was even more embarrassed when I looked at the packaging to discover that they were even slightly different in color and design.

I found what I was looking *for*, not what I was looking *at*. I was looking at two differently packaged pairs of socks and not seeing any difference. This is what we do in our lives. I call it a *mindset* disability. Our mind is set to see something and, often, it prevents us from seeing what we're looking *at*.

We would find more beauty and value in people if we look for them instead of looking for shortfalls, liabilities, and inadequacies. Imagine if everyone committed to looking for the good in the world, or, more importantly, in people (including and especially ourselves).

Do *you* know what you see or see what you know? ◆

Hold Your Judgment

To help people learn, I need to *be* "big enough" to tolerate whatever level of irritability they bring to class. This need is followed closely by the need to be *willing* to form a relationship with each of them – purposely. I must withhold judgment of every student's behavior and character if I hope to establish a healthy learning environment. Perhaps my best example of this came when I was teaching a class in Phoenix, AZ.

> ... to hold my judgment on anyone, especially those who tend to irritate me.

The class was like most others. The people were generally warm and kind with the average age being, I'd guess, about forty-three years. The youngest person in the class was rather impulsive and seemed quite self-serving. It appeared, early on, that he wasn't there to take the curriculum (personal growth) very seriously. He exuded an arrogant attitude and didn't engage or contribute to the small group discussions as others did. One of the mornings, he showed up an hour late and never said a word to me, or anyone else.

I admit this young man's attitude irritated me. In my years in personnel, I'd seen many like him. It was a major step in *my* personal growth, however, to understand the value and necessity of "masking" my feelings of irritation from people like him. To reveal my irritation would spoil the relationship I rely on to get the message through. Equally important to my teaching, I learned to refrain from focusing on the one or two people in class who don't seem serious. I carried on the sessions as normal and the class went great.

I asked for a personal evaluation at the end of class, and I want to share with you a couple of quotes from this young man's evaluation. "Thank you so much for teaching this class. It came at a time in my life when I needed to hear just what you are saying." "I can't wait to practice your teachings with my football team. I have the feeling I've been way too hard and inflexible with some of them."

I want to emphasize how good I feel about the lesson I learned: to hold my judgment on *anyone*, especially those who tend to irritate me. Outward appearance is usually a mask for what is happening inside. I am certain that, had I made a big deal of his attitude, had I made some kind of a point about his seeming cavalier behavior of coming in an hour late and not bothering to pay "homage to the professor," I would have destroyed the learning atmosphere between the student and the teacher. As his statements communicate, this young man gained from the experience. I could have ruined that by revealing my irritation, by judging him prematurely.

(Continued on next page)

Good Advice

I conclude that what I have discovered is not exclusive to the formal teaching and learning process. I believe it is just as true in the leadership arena, in the business arena, in the neighborhood and in the home.

The ability and willingness to build relationships is fundamental to a teacher's effectiveness. It usually requires refraining from judgments. ◆

The Last of Human Freedoms

In his famous book, *Man's Search for Meaning,* Viktor Frankl (Frankl 1987) detailed his horrifying experiences as a prisoner in a Nazi concentration camp during World War II. The basic premise of the book was, no matter what the Nazis did to or took away from their prisoners (food, freedom, dignity), they were unable to take away the prisoners' freedom to choose their response to what happened to them. That choice remained as the last of human freedoms.

> The last of human freedoms is to choose one's attitude in any given set of circumstances to choose one's own way.
>
> Vikor Frankl

I used to speak to middle school students about responsibility, and I recall throwing a harmless sponge ball at the face of two willing volunteers. One chose to put up her hands and stop the ball. The other (I had arranged with both of them ahead of time) left his hands to his side and allowed the ball to hit him in the face. I pointed out to the rest of the kids that each person had the choice to either put up his/her hands or not and that each should be willing to live with the consequences of his or her choice.

Far too many people who "leave their hands to their side," then go around whining to others about the ball hitting them in the face. Our lives are filled with choices, and we need to accept the consequences of those choices.

In my psychology training in college, I remember working with white rats. Most of the training of our rats depended on the fact that the poor creatures were always (purposely) thirsty. We had levers in their cages that delivered water to them when we decided. If a rat behaved a certain way, we gave it a drink of water. Soon, the rats would behave just as we wanted in order to get water.

One of the first things we learned was if a rat behaved in a certain way and did not receive a drink of water, it quit behaving that way. It was that simple. The rat didn't sit around and whine and cry about its cage, its handler or the world in general; it simply discontinued the unproductive behavior and busied itself in a way that might produce a satisfying reward. I think, "sometimes, if only we humans would act more like rats."

We don't need to search long to find people looking to blame someone else for conditions in their lives. Listen to them long enough and you'll hear a litany of

(Continued on next page)

changes they'd impose to make the world more suitable to them – to make their lives better. They seek to control everything in the world except the *one thing* they can control – their response to whatever happens to them.

We all seek contentment in our lives. If I am to be content, I need to accept the fact that I determine my response to anything that happens to me. Since I was given the ability to *make* choices, I am responsible for the *consequences* of them.

When a "ball hits me in the face," I am usually responsible.◆

Looking Backward

Today as I left my table at a local restaurant, I stopped briefly and looked back at the table and chairs. It took me less than five seconds to notice I left my reading glasses, so I picked them up. When I forget to pause and look, invariably, I leave something behind. This is a lesson for my life.

> **Most of the "stuff" in our lives is like the soiled dishes and utensils on the restaurant table.**

I believe I should leave most things behind me. Most of the "stuff" in our lives is like the soiled dishes and utensils on the restaurant table; we should learn to leave them behind.

What should be left behind is a legacy, a noble memory as an example to others. Creating this legacy means glancing back only to learn the lessons of the past. Our main focus needs to be forward.

As you move from point to point in your life, glance back and take with you only that which will benefit you in the future. Leave it neat, but leave most of it behind you. Your past (especially the hurt, pain and failure) exists in the only place possible – behind you and it is impossible to change it. Leave it there taking only from it the tools you need to build your future.

I need to remember to learn from the past and plan for the future but live in the present. ◆

Turn The Power Off And Clean Up
- hanging the tools where they belong

I read an article in *U.S.A. Today* that described the condition of children in the Silicon Valley of Northern California. It told of the torrid pace of life they experience as the young parents work to cash in on the fields of opportunity in the technology and microchip industry. "Children are being left to be raised by nannies, soccer coaches, dance teachers, schools and other outside agencies. Parents, in their attempt to substitute for themselves, are not only falling short of their responsibilities as parents but are engaging their youngsters in so many outside activities that there seems precious little time for kids (let alone their aspiring parents) to have any down time."

> We busy ourselves daily working right through "clean up."

I learned a lesson at a young age that helped me with the torrid pace life can take on. When I was in seventh grade, the boys took shop class and the girls took home economics (cooking and sewing). In the shop, all the tools were hung or placed neatly in the tool cage. Each day, following a few instructions from the teacher, we began working on our projects. I just loved shop class. It was right in my "wheelhouse."

With ten minutes left in the hour and most of us busy working on various electrical tools or machines, the power would go off. It was Mr. Cross (alias) at the switch, and he would bellow in his inimitable voice, "CLEAN UP!" Oh how we hated to stop what we were doing, especially to put away our tools and clean up.

I've come to believe this is a major shortfall of young and old alike today. We busy ourselves daily working right through "clean up." We don't stop to put things away where they belong – in the tool cages of our lives.

Shop class may hold a lesson for the children and adults in Silicon Valley. Today's stimulation-filled world seems to encourage us to keep going right through the "clean up" of our lives.

In my own life, I am much happier if I allow the time to "turn off the power and clean up." Putting my clothing away and selecting my clothing for the next day is often the *last* thing I want to do at night. I prefer to simply exit my clothing and jump into bed. *However* distasteful as this may be at night, it is "nearly indigestible" to face a mess the next morning and the chore of selecting my attire. What a psychological boost to begin my day with "all my tools hanging neatly in their place." ◆

The Emperor's New Clothes

Late in my educational career, I decided to become a middle school principal and leave my work in the central office. I did so because I wanted to get back to working closer to children. When children violate the simple rules of respect, I find I am more understanding and tolerant than when adults do the same. I feel adults have had plenty of time to develop rules of respect, whereas kids have not.

> "Hey look, that guy's naked!"

My experience with adult groups is that they tend to engage in what George Orwell (in his book, "1984"), termed, "Groupthink." They sacrifice scrutiny of ideas for harmony and unanimity. They seek group peace and accord so they avoid the oft-painful process of open examination of their actions and decisions. They avoid the conflict that often accompanies a thorough examination of the various functions of the group. This is dangerous.

In the famous children's story, *"The Emperor's New Clothes"* it took a small child to announce the fact that the emperor was striding down the street without clothing. It took a child to go against the group harmony, unanimity and safety of similar thought to say, "Hey look, that guy's naked!" With the display of courage (naiveté actually), everyone acknowledged the king's misfortune and embarrassment.

I recall times I stood mute as I saw an "emperor striding right down the middle of the street, completely naked" as our group pretended he was "fully clothed." Don't be too hard on yourself if you stood mute as you saw the same thing. It happens at the highest levels of decision-making in the world.

In the Bay of Pigs morass (see *The Shirt and Tie Illusion*), President Kennedy was led into an ill-fated decision in Cuba by a cabinet of advisors who chose group harmony and deference to the president over coming out and saying, "Hey, that guy is naked." Perhaps we ought to include children in some of our major decisions – at all levels! ◆

The Burden Of Judgment

There are various interpretations of the Biblical story of Adam and Eve in the Garden of Eden. According to the Christian Bible, they were the first of God's human creation. The variety of explanations of this parable's metaphoric meaning is as vast as the number of "experts" who have sought to illuminate it. The interpretation that makes the most sense to me is written by Alan Cohen in his book, *I Had It All The Time*. (Cohen 1996) He relates the story of Adam and Eve to judgment.

According to Cohen in his interpretation, God created humans (Adam and Eve) and placed them in the Garden of Eden. This beautiful garden is the metaphoric equivalent of the Kingdom of God with all of the beauty, peace, harmony and plentiful bounty available to humans. The wisest are those who seek to enjoy this beauty, peace, harmony and plentiful bounty – every day.

> **Shed the burden of judgment**

"Eat not from but one of the lovely trees in the garden," God cautioned Adam and Eve. He meant the tree of the knowledge of good and evil. This tree was the one that bore the fruit that, if eaten, would burden humans with the ability to pass judgment as to what is good and what is evil. Further, this perpetual "need" to pass judgment serves mostly to impede us from living in and enjoying the Garden that, again, is all the beauty, peace, harmony and plentiful bounty God created for us. The consequence of judgment is exclusion from the Kingdom of God.

Deepak Chopra says we need to "shed the burden of judgment." Passing judgment on others is a burdensome task many seem to shoulder with ignorance of its consequences.

I read what Chopra said about judgment years ago and only recently Cohen's interpretation of the Eden story. I now realize the meaning of the sin of eating from the tree of knowledge. It is sinful to sit in judgment of the good and evil of other people. I have enough to do simply to judge my own behavior, holding it up to the model and standard set by Buddha, Christ, Mohammed and all the other revered religious icons.

So it goes. Many of us spend our days in the judgment of what is good and what is evil. Most of the time we are judging other people, their behaviors, their possessions, their abilities, etc. This is hard work that requires a lot of attention. It is indeed a burden. As we busy ourselves judging, we are, unknowingly, distancing ourselves further and further from God's vast Kingdom.

(Continued on next page)

I had a difficult time reconciling my beliefs about judgment and my profession. I spent over 30 years in public education, most of which was in administration. Because of my work in personnel and as a principal, I was called upon continually to pass judgment on employees. It was my job to determine the "good and bad" of employee value in the classroom and elsewhere.

Had I judged their work as bad ("evil"), I had to do what I could to either change them or sever their employment. I reconciled my profession with my beliefs, reasoning that someone is also judging *me* professionally. That is how it should be. I was trained to recognize quality (good) for the children of the world in the forum of their education. I believe I was doing God's work by using my talents to ensure that His children receive the best education, training and upbringing that the public schools could provide. This work was different than the personal and subjective judgments I might make of people when I don't need to. This judgment is a burden and I am "eating from the wrong tree!" I could be spending this time in the "Kingdom of God." ◆

The Will And The Knowledge
- what I know and what I do

I watched an interview with the father of a girl who was kicked off her college basketball team for drinking and partying too much. He wondered why she did such a thing. "She knew better," he said, "I told her hundreds of times about the consequences of partying."

It happened because there is a difference between *knowing* something and *doing* (or refraining from doing) it. My ability to control my reaction to something is my emotional control and it has little to do with my knowledge.

> **The notion that an infusion of knowledge will inspire people to action is one of mankind's greatest misconceptions .**
> Hacker's Law

It only seems logical that knowing something will enable us to do it. This is one of the biggest misconceptions of mankind according to Hacker's law (see insert). Knowledge doesn't guarantee action. Action requires *will*. In our information/knowledge-based world, it's too bad there is so little emphasis on *will* and, especially, on "extending oneself." As I indicated in an earlier message, these are the two major components of love. For refreshment: *Love is the will to extend oneself for one's own and another person's spiritual growth.*

I *know* the right foods to eat. This doesn't insure I *will* always eat them. I have the *knowledge* of how useless a chocolate bar is to me, but I often lack the *will* to forego the pleasure. Foregoing the pleasure is, to varying degrees, the biggest challenge most people face. We lack the will to live our lives as our knowledge tells us. Our surrender to our desires often leads us down a path of personal disappointment if not destruction. "I know I should exercise but I can't," sounds almost like a prayer, a plea for help from those whose lives have become a series of losses to their own desires.

The strength to forego comes from somewhere deep inside a person. I believe I am better off having this strength than all the *knowledge* in the world as, nowhere in the definition of love is the word "knowledge" even implied.

Oh, the power of love. ◆

Finding Comfort In Who We Are?

Our lives seem to be a series of events that take place in a world filled with things (material) and people. Most of us form our beliefs about who we are based on what others say we are. Sometimes, our "self" becomes our body parts. Lessons such as, "Did you wipe your *self*" after our first attempts at potty training and "Make your *self* look ten years younger with XYZ facial cream," gave us the impression that we are our body.

Some of us were even called by such names as "peach, sunshine and honey." Sometimes, we were called other body parts that I can't mention in "G-rated" work! Despite these descriptions of who we are, our physical body is not *who* we are! We err when we determine who we are through the judgments of other people, television commercials or romantic and idealistic Hollywood fantasies. You see, who you are is not physically or materially defined. It is not a product of the judgment of others. Who you are is spiritual. It is deep inside and you are the only person who even can know for sure who that might be.

> **The intent of most marketing is to make us uncomfortable with who we are.**

Self-identity is critical to our spiritual health. Commercials designed to market products (get our money) are shoved in our faces in various forms. We're bombarded with unrealistic models of who we should try to be. Consumerism barrages us with messages designed to convince us we don't look good enough, run fast enough, drive a big enough car or wear stylish enough clothing. The intent of most marketing is to make us uncomfortable with *who* we are. Spending *your* money on *their* product will help you feel comfortable with who you are, but you can never really be comfortable for long as you'd no longer need their product. God forbid, what would they do without your money? New ways need to be devised to make us feel uncomfortable.

People displayed in commercials, Hollywood movies and other forms of advertising are not reality. Most people are incapable of looking or acting like the models. The key words are "looking" and "acting." Both imply illusions, not reality.

In reality, many of these models are illusions whose own lives are often twisted and painful because they are void of knowledge of who they are. So many of their personal lives spiral downward into a pitiful heap of broken marriages, drug-filled experiences and confused children who also struggle with who they are.

(Continued on next page)

Some of these revered models exist in a race of endless comparisons, judgments and contests obscuring their ability to look inside to see who they are, spiritually. Their world requires them to be the wealthiest, best looking and most successful. Who they are is nearly totally defined by outside standards – someone else's standards. Despite this, many continue to pursue the elusive vision portrayed by the media. Every effort spent doing this is wasted – an hour that could be used in our own search for self.

I believe I am *what I do*, every day. My actions are a product of my beliefs, abilities and will to act. Actions are a reflection of what I think. Everything begins with a thought and I choose my thoughts. I reveal my thoughts through my actions. This fortifies my belief that *I am what I do.*

In deciding who we are, it is best to get alone and go inside. Begin by discovering your natural gifts and talents as therein lay your greatest potential. Therein are the most powerful tools available to help you accomplish your purpose in life. Discover them, decide *who* you are and begin your unique mission on earth. Most people never do. One of the saddest facts I ever heard is how much of this natural talent and ability lies in the hills of the local graveyard. ◆

Falling Through The Cracks

The Macinac Bridge in Michigan is five miles long in the winter and up to five miles and one foot long in the heat of the summer. Millions of cars have crossed the bridge since its opening in 1958. Not one of these cars has fallen through any cracks in the bridge because there has never been a crack in the bridge that would allow a car to fall through. The bridge itself expands and contracts, with seasonal changes, up to one foot per year. Expansion joints are strategically placed along the bridge to create the flexibility necessary for the bridge to accommodate its (seasonally) "different size."

Imagine you are sitting in your living room and you notice a draft coming through your wall. You go outside to examine it and discover two things: the wind is blowing very hard and there is a crack in the wall of your house. It is humorous to think that you might try to slow the wind or switch its direction. Of course you begin thinking how you might fix the crack in the wall.

> "Why do we continue to focus on changing kids if the cracks are in the system?"

In my years in public education, one expression that has survived is "falling through the cracks." It is used to describe kids who are failing school for various reasons.

Where are the cracks? Are the cracks in the kids? The cracks are in the system, of course. Then who has charge of designing the system and where are the "expansion joints" in it?

We (the professionals) are in charge of the system. If cars began falling through cracks in the Macinac Bridge, would system engineers begin working on the cars? Why, then, do some believe that we are going to keep kids from falling through the cracks by expecting changes in the kids? We need to design a system with the flexibility to educate every child to the best of his or her ability.

Children are people and people are like the wind. You and I can't change people any more than we can change the direction of the wind. We can alter the system (schools or other) that we "process" people through, but never, I want to repeat this, *never* are we able to change people. The only person that can change me, is me. The same goes for you.

W. Edwards Deming (principal architect of Japan's post war economic re-building) said, "Don't blame the workers." He was speaking of factories when

(Continued on next page)

production levels went "south." He went on to explain that management controls eighty-five percent of the decisions made in production, so how could the workers be blamed when something goes wrong. To blame are the people who design the system (management). It is convenient to blame the workers, but it is erroneous.

I believe Deming's findings apply to schools. It is the professionals who control eighty-five percent of the decisions made in the educational system. If kids are falling through the cracks, and the cracks are in the system, we need to get busy repairing the cracks and installing expansion joints to allow flexibility in an increasingly complex, ever-changing society. Children have no decision-making authority. Let us stop trying to change the wind – or blame it for whistling through the crack in our wall. ◆

Who Packs Your Parachute?

I'm no hero

In my work as a middle school principal, I found it easy to imagine that there were future teachers, construction workers, business owners, attorneys, doctors, parents, leaders, etc. in our hallways. Ten to twenty years hence, these adolescents will become the bulk of our workforce, as we adults will be off enjoying retirement. That's the way it has always been. It's not unusual for some people to hold the view that they (or their work) are more important than others. Money and status have become our measure of importance.

Years ago, I heard a former jet fighter pilot (and POW) from the Vietnam War speak. His speech had the same title as his book, *I'm No Hero* (Plumb 1983). I recall a particular part of his talk that always held special meaning to me. It reminded me that, whatever I do in this world, I should never consider it more important than the work of anyone else.

Who Packs Your Parachute?

Daily routine can blind us to what (and who) is really important in life. We may fail to say hello, please, or thank you, or some other courtesy. We neglect giving compliments when due, or simply being respectful and friendly for no reason. In his book, Lt. Plumb tells a story, "Who Packs Your Parachute?" I hope you find the same meaning and caution in it as I did.

Lt. Charles Plumb, a US Naval Academy graduate, was a jet fighter pilot in Vietnam. After seventy-five combat missions, his plane was destroyed by a surface-to-air missile. Plumb ejected and parachuted into enemy hands. He spent six years in a Communist Vietnamese prison. He survived the ordeal and began lectures on lessons learned from the experience. He became somewhat famous for his speaking and message.

As he tells it, one day after his return, he and his wife were sitting in a restaurant when a man from another table came up and said, "You're Lt. Plumb! You flew jet fighters in Vietnam from the aircraft carrier Kitty Hawk. You were shot down!"

"How in the world did you know that?" asked Plumb.

"I packed your parachute," the man replied. Plumb gasped in surprise and gratitude.

The man pumped his hand and said, "I guess the chute worked!" Plumb assured him, "It sure did. If your chute hadn't worked, I wouldn't be here today."

(Continued on next page)

Plumb couldn't sleep that night, thinking about the man. "I kept wondering what he might have looked like in a Navy uniform – a Dixie cup hat, a bib in the back, and bell bottom trousers. I wonder how many times I might have seen him and not even said good morning, how are you or anything because, you see, I was a fighter pilot and he was just a sailor," regretted Plumb.

He thought of the many hours the sailor had spent on a long wooden table in the bowels of the ship, carefully weaving the shrouds and folding the silks of each chute, holding in his hands each time the fate of someone he didn't know.

Now, Plumb asks his audience, "Who's packing your parachute? Everyone has someone who provides what's necessary to make it through the day. Are you walking by him or her without notice?"

Plumb also points out that he needed many kinds of parachutes when his plane was shot down over enemy territory; he needed his physical parachute, his mental parachute, his emotional parachute and his spiritual parachute. He called on all these supports before reaching safety. His experience reminds us all to prepare ourselves to weather whatever storms lie ahead and be grateful to those who work to help us through.

As you go through this week, month, year, recognize those people who pack YOUR parachute! ◆

Rushing The Passer

I love the story of the young lad that wanted to learn everything his maharishi (wise teacher) knew. He pressed the maharishi for how long it would take to learn it all. The old master had a difficult time answering that question but finally said, "Okay, it would take you about ten years." "But what if I quit my job, stay up late at night, work extra hard and dedicate all of my time to learning what you know. Then how long would it take me?" the young student asked. "Twenty years," replied the sage.

I was the quarterback of my high school football team. I was a great passer. That is if you were on the other team, because most of my passes ended up in the arms of an opponent. I recall telling my coach, after an interception, that I could pass a lot better if I didn't feel so rushed. I saw no call for humor, but my coach just laughed at me.

> **A child is born when she is ready.**
> **A child crawls when she is ready.**
> **A child walks when she is ready.**
> **A child talks when she is ready.**
> **When she's five, she goes to school.**

In football, it is a deliberate strategy to rush the passer. When hurried, he is more likely to make a mistake. I believe hurrying is true in life as well as football. I recall my elementary teachers placing a big clock in front of the class and "warning" that we had thirty minutes to finish a test. My mind would go blank and still would today!

With fifty-plus years of living experience (thirty in the field of public education), I continue to be confused as to why we rush children in the learning process. Why do we have timed tests in school? Why does the teacher snap her fingers as the second grader struggles with the multiplication tables? Rushing causes mistakes, period.

Daniel Goleman (1985) explains that learning something new requires total attention. Jimmy Johnson, famous football coach, didn't yell at or discipline a player who was learning something new because it impedes learning. With all this evidence, I'm confused as to why we continue to rush children as they learn. It is difficult to change, it is a lot of work and it takes time.

Still, rapid learning does have significance. We have all experienced things that we seem to "pick up" quickly and easily. It happens when we have natural ability to do something. It may be physical, mental or even mystical – but it merely indicates a natural ability to perform.

(Continued on next page)

Good Advice

There is *never* a classroom of children who all have the same abilities. Therefore, the learning process should never be rushed. The great virtuoso Michelangelo said, "If people knew the millions of hours I spent practicing, they would never call me a genius." Patience and time on task, the will to practice, determine greatness. The process can't be rushed.

Rushing the passer causes mistakes....by design!! Take your time and give all the time necessary for *learning* to happen. ◆

The Power Of Teachers
- and understanding

I want to begin by telling the end of a story. "I would like to attend the trainings," the young player explained, "but I have to work extra hours to help my mom support our family. Our father left us and we need the money." The coach excused him from further weight-training sessions and welcomed him back to the team. Somewhere, in Ohio, a 17-year-old boy got a break from his coach. Now the *beginning* of the story.....

> - parenting and teaching are practically identical.

I was teaching a class in attitude and getting to know the students, as I always try to do. It is rare, but this particular class had a young man in it that seemed the "coach type."

I've learned not to rely on my first impression of others, since I've been guilty of inaccurately portraying my own personality and character, and I dislike it when others make hasty judgments about me. This young coach radiated an attitude of indifference to the rest of the class. Some people take my classes simply to gain credit so they can move up on the pay schedule. He appeared to be one of these, not there to learn or contribute but just gain the graduate credit with little expenditure of energy.

Throughout the weekend, the young coach didn't contribute much to the group discussions. This seemed to confirm my original evaluation of his character. His exterior was rough, tough and challenging. As a competitor, he could show no weakness, of course.

Earlier in my career, this type of student would have bothered me. I'm thankful I have overcome that. Whatever his personality or character, I had twenty-seven other students who would not know the real Craig Schmidt had I allowed this one student to affect me. A big component in a teacher's effectiveness is how well the students know him/her. Had I challenged him, or his attitude in any way, I would have served no purpose for the class and would only have alienated him. I continued to treat him as I treated everyone else.

Strangely, as I passed out my end-of-class evaluations, I was one short. The coach volunteered to pass on the evaluation, which appeared consistent with the rest of his attitude that weekend. To my surprise, he took out a piece of paper and began to write. When he finished, he put his writing in the evaluations folder.

(Continued on next page)

Good Advice

The next morning, at a coffee shop, I began reading the evaluations. Among them was a letter from the "chip-on-the-shoulder" coach. I had tears in my eyes as I read what he wrote. He explained he thought I was a great teacher who came into his life at a time he needed it. He said he had to soften up a little in his approach to people. The class work we did on understanding others had specific meaning to him.

A week later, he submitted the required project along with another short note. Again, he thanked me for the job I did and explained the story (football player). The young man had missed a lot of weight lifting sessions and he (coach) had enough, so he cut him without bothering to find out the reasons for his absences.

The Monday after class, the coach called the player into his office for a talk. He explained to him he had cut him since he hadn't made the required number of weight-training sessions. This time, however, he bothered to ask the reason for the absences. The young man explained.......(see end of story above).

Some 17-year-old kid in Ohio got a break from his coach. I believe this likely would not have happened had I challenged or otherwise alienated this coach in class. Had I done this, he may have tuned out completely and never absorbed the lesson in understanding. The break this young boy received is one he will likely remember for the rest of his life.

Herein lies the power of teachers. As a teacher, *it is my job* to establish good relationships with all of my students – to accept them for *what, when and where* they are in their development.

When the teacher accepts and understands the student, the student is likely to mimic the treatment. Therefore, accepting students for who and what they are is the most important thing teachers do, or don't do. This is probably the same with parents, as parenting and teaching are practically identical. ◆

I Need Help

As I sat in the Burger King in Dowagiac, Michigan working on my writing, I noticed a man walk by with several bags. I "profiled" (yes, we all profile) him to be homeless! I felt sympathy as he appeared lonely, tired and hungry.

A short time later, I noticed he was sitting at a table near me and had a cup of coffee with several packets of sugar. I felt even more sorry for him after a close-up look. I had an urge to offer to buy him a sandwich but didn't. He was in the restaurant but a short time before leaving.

A half hour later, I looked up and saw him, again, meandering around in the parking lot. This time, there were two elderly gentlemen in the dining room playing a game. One of them saw this person and said to his friend, "Now, there's a pathetic sight. I think I'll buy him a sandwich." He approached the man outside, came inside and purchased a bacon cheeseburger and delivered it to the man.

> "Now there's a pathetic sight."

I wonder if he would have been given a sandwich had he not *looked* so pathetic. I wonder how many impoverished souls walk by me every day but they don't look impoverished. Their pain and condition is far worse than the man on the street. They are facing fractured relationships, loss of loved ones, financial stress and a myriad of other problems that cannot be profiled because they appear to be okay. So many of them could use a "sandwich" of my time, sympathy or empathetic ear.

Looking impoverished will get you all the sandwiches you need, and more. *Being* impoverished won't necessarily get you any attention. This doesn't mean you don't need it; you simply don't *appear* to need it. You *appear* okay.

Today's fast-paced, competitive, consumeristic society creates thousands of impoverished souls. It's a sign of weakness to show this so we don masks in order appear strong. Few of us want to appear weak. Unfortunately, the result is pent-up frustration, want, need, etc., and they take their toll on our spirit.

Sometimes we need to *look* impoverished to get a "sandwich." It's our personal responsibility to communicate our level of impoverishment before we end up on the street – alone. Asking for help shouldn't require a masquerade. I need to learn to simply ask. ◆

Then Providence Moves Too
My last chapter – by design

Since I decided I was going to write and publish a book, I've noticed how many people who say they'd like to write a book or they should write one. I guess most feel they are incapable of composing anything worth reading, just as I did.

When I *said* I was going to publish my book, many people expressed an interest in reading it. Further, when I decided *how* I was going to publish it (basically self-publishing at the local Kinkos store), "Providence" moved with me. A woman who took both of my classes works with a woman whose husband is a writer.

After some coaxing, I met with the writer. We hit it off and he affirmed my work. This inspired me. Beyond that, he has connections to a small publishing company that not only beat Kinkos' price, they saved me hours of work and wasted time. I'm convinced the woman who prodded me is an agent of Providence and likely has no idea that she is.

> Fear is almost always the obstacle to commitment.

I always kind of believed in Providence. The book in your hands sealed that belief. What I didn't realize, and what the people who *say* they should write a book don't realize, is that the "lynchpin" between the wagon and the engine of success is *commitment to do something*. A firm commitment is what is needed to enlist the power of Providence. Fear is almost always the obstacle to commitment. All I want to communicate here is a quote by Emerson, "Do the thing you fear and the death of fear is certain."

To drop the lynchpin between the tongue of the wagon and engine of success, you must overcome fear (mostly fear of rejection) and commit yourself to your future.

It merits repeating the words of mountain climber William Hutchins Murray here:

"Concerning acts of initiative or creation, there is one elementary truth, the ignorance of which kills countless ideas and splendid plans: that the moment one definitely commits oneself, then Providence moves too."

As I indicated in the title, it is by design I chose this as my final chapter. I did this because, in my teaching, I find so many people who would like to change. So many who would like to utilize their talents to grow. So many who would like to risk and can't. To all of them my message is simple – "Do something." Make

(Continued on next page)

yourself do one little thing today and every day, no matter how little. You will be shocked at the forms Providence takes to move you along.

Providence is a tremendously beneficial force that moves in many, sometimes strange, ways. However, to get it to move, you have to move – first. There is a huge force out there waiting for you to "Do something." ◆

References

Barry D. *Dave Barry Turns 40,* New York: Ballantine Books, 1990

Bedarraco, J. *Leading Quietly,* National Public Radio Live Interview, 2002

Cameron, J. *The Right to Write,* New York: Putnam Publishing, 1999

Carnegie, D *How To Win Friends And Influence People,* New York: Simon & Schuster, 1981

Chopra, D. *Ageless Body Timeless Mind,* New York: Harmony Books, 1993

Clifton, D. *Soar With Your Strengths,* New York: Bantam Doubleday, 1992

Clifton, D. *Interview,* founder/*CEO of Selection Research Incorporated,* Lincoln, NE (Now Gallup Polls), June 1991

Cohen, A. *I Had It All The Time,* Kuala Lumpur, Malaysa: Synergy Book International, 1996

Covey, S. *The 7 Habits of Highly Effective People,* New York: Simon and Schuster, 1989

Covey, S. *First Things First,* New York: Simon and Schuster, 1994

Decker, B. *You've Got To Be Believed To Be Heard,* New York: St. Martin's Press, 1992

Edelman, M. *The Measure of Our Success,* New York: Harper Perennial, 1992

Farson, R. *Management of the Absurd,* New York: Touchstone, 1996

Frankl V. *Man's Search For Meaning,* Boston: Beacon Press, 1992

Grand Rapids {MI} *Press Brain and Stomach in the Battle to Control Your Bulge* 11/28/02

Goleman, D. *Emotional Intelligence,* New York: Bantam, 1995

Goleman, D. *Vital Lies, Simple Truths,* New York: Simon and Schuster, 1985

Hamer and Copeland *Living With Our Genes,* New York: Doubleday, 1998

Jamieson, K. *An Unquiet Mind,* New York: Vintage Books, 1995

Kohn, A. *No Contest,* New York: Houghton Mifflin, 1994

Kaltman, A. *Cigars, Whiskey & Winning Leadership Lessons from Gen. Ulysses S. Grant,* NJ: Prentice Hall, 1998

Likona, T. *Raising Good Children,* New York: Bantam Books, 1994

Mahoney, D. *Confessions Of A Street Smart Manager,* New York: Simon & Schuster, 1988

Palmer, P. *The Courage to Teach,* San Francisco: Jossey-Bass, 1998

Peck, M.S. *The Road Less Traveled,* New York: Touchstone, 1978

Peck, M.S. *Further Along The Road Less Traveled,* New York: Simon and Schuster, 1983

Plumb, C. *I'm No Hero,* Missouri: Independence Press, 1983

Note: To view a more complete list of readings suggested by Craig Schmidt, visit his website www.pcinstitute.net and click on the *bibliography link.*

To order additional copies of *Good Advice*,
go to our website

www.pcinstitute.net